Bringing up your Parents

A GUIDE FOR TEENAGERS

John Farman

Illustrated by Kathryn Lamb

PICCADILLY PRESS • LONDON

First published under the title of *Keep Out of the Reach of Parents!*
by Piccadilly Press Ltd in 1992
This fully revised and expanded edition first published 2005
by Piccadilly Press Ltd,
5 Castle Road, London NW1 8PR
www.piccadillypress.co.uk

A catalogue record for this book is available from the British Library

ISBN: 1 85340 846 8 (trade paperback)
EAN: 9 781853 408465

3 5 7 9 10 8 6 4 2

Printed and bound in Great Britain by Bookmarque Ltd
Cover illustration by John Farman. Cover design by Louise Millar.
Text design by Textype Typesetters
Set in Stempel Garamond

Papers used by Piccadilly Press are produced from forests grown and
managed as a renewable resource, and which conform to the
requirements of recognised forestry accreditation schemes.

CONTENTS

Why This Book and Why Now?

Way back in 1992, when hardly anyone had mobile phones and Princess Diana decided she didn't want to be queen, I wrote the first version of this book. At the time, I thought teenagers seemed to be getting the blame for everything and it just didn't seem fair. There had been loads of books written for parents, telling them what was wrong with their kids, and advising them how best to deal with them, but as far as I could tell, there were none to help the subject of their grief – you lot. Why couldn't teenagers have a book, I asked myself, telling them what was wrong with their parents for a change? Although that first book's now well out of date, you'll be pleased to know, in some respects, nothing's changed – you're still getting the blame for everything.

Some of the things I deal with may not concern you,

but I bet most will. If you sail through life, however, and your parents think you're perfect, or worse, you think you're perfect, then return this book from wherever you got it, and get back to your PlayStation forthwith. Alternatively, you might have parents who are child psychologists, and think you might not need my advice. Forget it. Most psychologists I've ever known have been round the bend themselves, so you'll probably need this book more than most.

We all know that teenagers can be a pain in the bum – it's sort of expected somehow, but what parents seem conveniently to forget is that you're having to cope with so many things at once: school, homework, changes to the way you think, changes to your body, your feelings towards the opposite sex and, much more to the point ... THEM.

Why *do* they make it so difficult? Weren't they ever teenagers? Didn't they ever have days when World War Three seemed a better alternative to getting out of bed, or look in the mirror only to find their faces had turned into spot farms overnight? Didn't they have days when they didn't want to talk to anyone except the goldfish, and did they really come from the Planet Perfect, like they'd have you believe?

Being a teenager is tricky at the best of times, but

being a fully paid-up, no-excuses-for-nothing adult in this millennium is seldom much fun either (I should know). It's tempting to compare what happens when you grow up and grow old to climbing a vast mountain. You climb and climb the damn thing for what seems ever, until eventually you get to the top, but then what? You sit around for a few moments, get well bored . . . and then start the long trek down again.

The trouble with growing up is that you never know where the top is, or even whether you've reached it – until one day you realise you're sliding, hell for leather, down the other side.

Wouldn't it be great if we could all reach a kind of brilliant plateau where not only do you look your best, but have lots of your own money, oodles of self-confidence . . . and no spots! A time when no one asks you questions every five minutes or expects you to do things you don't want . . . and a time when you can afford your mobile bill!

Why Me?

So what, you may ask, qualifies me to write this book? I'm obviously not a teenager, and I'm obviously not still a parent of a teenager, because, if I was, I'd not have a clue what I was talking about. No, my kids are now grown up and luckily I've been able to talk with them about what it was like having me as a dad when they were your age. One good thing about being neither a parent of a teenager nor a teenager myself any more, is that I can look at the whole thing in a much more distanced way – but still see things from both sides of the fence. Who knows, maybe I might be able to help someone who's going through it now?

Warning!

This book is for you and you only. When you have finished it, you might want to swallow it page by page, lest the dreaded 'Them Downstairs' get hold of it.

CHAPTER ONE
Home(work) and Away
When School and Parents Just Don't Mix

One aspect of the parental point of view that really gets up your nose is when they try the old 'You're so lucky' line. Parents, by their very nature, always believe their kids have it easier than they did. This line usually comes out when you suggest that you might not want to go on to A-levels, or when you want to go travelling, or if you reject anything that might end up in a job. Most times, they'd rather have you in a safe, secure job than have you risk doing anything that might be exciting or remotely enjoyable. The most ghastly thing is that you could well find yourself saying the same thing when you're in the same position.

Sometimes, there is pressure to follow in your parents'

footsteps. If your dad is successful in what he does, he might not be able to comprehend why you could possibly not want to go into the same profession. If he went to university, he will more than likely want you to do the same. My dad worked in the City of London as an insurance broker. When I told him I wanted to go to art school and never wear a suit and tie, he nearly blew a gasket. (But guess who won that particular argument in the end . . . ?)

Given all this, it's no wonder parents get so agitated when it comes to following your education . . .

Homework

Unless you're a fully paid-up swot, homework and exam revision are going to be among the worst chores you're ever going to endure. It's bad enough having to do schoolwork all day, without having to think about it *after* school as well.

Just mention 'homework' and the best of households usually break into a cold war. You can tell your parents that you're doing enough work till you're blue in the face, but do they believe you? I'm sorry, but they'd be more likely to believe you if you said you felt like doing the washing-up for a month. Here's the stupid, non-productive sort of chat a daughter might have with her father:

Father: And where exactly do you think you're going? *(The famous old war-cry.)* Have you finished all your homework?

Teenager: Don't panic, Dad. We've got a free period tomorrow morning – I can finish it then. *(Since when have they called a ten-minute bus ride a free period?)*

Father: When I was your age, I realised how important education was – and we had twice the home-work you seem to get.

Teenager (under breath): Surely he's not going to say he wouldn't have got where he is today if he hadn't studied . . .

Father: Look, it might seem a waste of time now, but wait until you try and get a job – they don't grow on trees, you know. *(What about fruit-picking?)*

Teenager: Look, I'm only going round to Charlie's for half an hour. I doubt that's going to ruin my whole future. *(Now is the time to smile sweetly and head for the door.)*

Father: You've never been round there for 'only half an hour' in your life. Don't go blaming me when you fail your exams. Look, I'm not going to say all this again. *(If you believe that, you'll believe anything.)*

Teenager (under breath): If only that were true. I spend more time arguing about homework than actually doing it.

Parent's View

I used to hate being nagged when I was a kid, but I'm so glad I listened. I'm sure youngsters these days don't have a clue how tough it is out there to get a job in the adult world. If I had my teenage years again, I'd work twice as hard. All she seems to be interested in is clothes, boys and music. Fat lot of good they'll do her when she's trying to get her head round an exam paper or struggling through her first job interview.

Teenager's View

If they gave prizes for persistence, Dad would score big time. I've heard all that do-as-I-did stuff so many times I practically say it in my sleep. Anyway, what's the big deal about a good job – for a start, there aren't any, and anyway, I'm not so sure I want one if I'm going to end up as grumpy as him. According to his all-knowingness, if I fail a single GCSE, I'll be cast into eternal damnation (probably with all those dumb books). I just wish he'd stop getting so steamed up over things that are, when you really think about it, none of his business. If only he'd leave it to me, I'm sure I'll do better if I do it my own way.

How to Handle Your Parents

1. 'Not yet' is a diplomatic (and truthful) answer to enquiries after your progress, but could lead to further badgering. Tell them there's plenty of time until you have to hand it in. Your version of 'plenty' might be different from theirs.

2. Just say, 'Yes', then invite them to read your essay on the socio-political ramifications of the Canadian logging industry. That should put them off (unless one of them is a lumberjack).

3. Tell them that you're working on it with a friend and that you need to go round to discuss it (that, and television and clothes and who's seeing who in school . . .).

4. Say that the latest scientific study says that in order for the human brain to work at its optimum ability, one needs plenty of sleep (also serves as an excuse for staying in bed late at weekends or having a nap in your room when you get home from school instead of doing your homework).

5. Create a homework timetable. This will give the impression that you fully intend to do some work –

and, if you plan it cleverly, that you are in the middle of a study break. (A homework timetable can also potentially be very helpful if you actually *do* some work.)

School Reports

If I'd been able to multiply the number of times my school reports said *'could have done better'* with the number of times it said *'minimal attention span'*, I might have passed my maths exams. I always thought these were pretty stupid remarks anyway. Of *course* I could have done better. Even the cleverest, creepiest person in the school could have done better. Apart from pointing this out to your parents and saying that you think your teachers have got you mixed up with someone else, there's very little you can do. If they really go off on one, however, you could try asking to see some of their old school reports. Chances are, if you take after them in any way, theirs won't have been much better.

Parents' Evening

The up-side to going to school is that you get to spend time away from your parents, but inevitably your paths will cross.

Parent–teacher meetings aren't so bad, as long as yours is the kind of school where the students get to attend the appointments too. Teachers usually bend over backwards to be nice at these meetings. They have to try and think of nice things to say about the wonderful progress you're making. Let's face it: if you're not learning anything, your mum and dad will probably think it's their fault.

PARENTS' EVENING

As for the big end-of-term events, I'll always remember one of my daughter's speech days in particular. It was the only time she'd ever wanted me there and it was because she was getting a prize. It was a hot day, as I remember, and I decided to wear a pale linen suit, thinking this would be appropriate. As I entered the school hall, the general consensus amongst my daughter and her friends (whose parents were dressed far more conservatively) was that I looked like a South American drug dealer.

If your parents are in any way likely to embarrass you – not just by what they wear: maybe they laugh like seals or constantly trip over their own (and everyone else's) feet – then don't let them near your school. If your schoolmates are anything like mine were, or my daughter's, you won't ever hear the end of it.

Final Thoughts . . .

Our education seems to happen at exactly the wrong time in our lives. There are always more exciting things to do – things that certainly don't involve having your nose stuck in a flipping book. Wouldn't it be great if we could do our studying when we're really old – there's hardly anything else worth doing then!

CHAPTER TWO

Put It Away
(So What's the Big Deal With Being Tidy?)

> **Note:** if your room looks like an IKEA showroom with everything exactly in its right place, then skip this chapter.

When God created the world, it was probably dead untidy, with things like rocks, trees, lakes and amoebas all over the place. Tidiness is a man-made, or rather, parent-made concept and it is totally unnecessary. It's also often impossible to perfect, and all teenagers can ever strive for to be is tidy *enough*. The following conversation might ring a bell:

Mother: Have you done something about your room yet? It looks like there's been a riot in there.

Teenager: Ha very ha. Anyway, what's the big problemo?

You don't have to live in it – I do. If anything, you should feel sorry for me.

Mother: I feel sorrier for the family of rats I saw moving out holding their noses. *(Hmm! Not a bad joke for an adult.)*

Teenager: Look, Mum, I know where everything is, so what's the big deal?

Mother: I only went in the other day because the whole household had run out of mugs. I couldn't find my way back to the door.

Teenager: You didn't come across my pet alligator did you? Look, I'll do it on Saturday, I promise. *(Ancient Chinese proverb: Always put off today what you might not even get round to tomorrow.)*

Mother: I'll believe it when I see it. You wait till you've got a place of your own and there's no one else to tidy up after you. *(What about the servants?)*

Parent's View

Every time I try to sort his room out, he seems to try even harder to turn it into a municipal tip. The trouble is, I've always done far too much for those kids. I should go on strike – they'd soon complain then, I bet, when they can't find clean socks to wear.

Teenager's View

Jeez, she's like one of those battery ads – you know, the ones that have toys that go on and on and on . . . She's the one that never runs out. If I could charge my mum for each time she goes on about my room, I'd be able to buy a house of my own . . . and pay a cleaner. Why does it get up *her* nose so much? I don't go around the rest of the house complaining because it's too tidy, do I? The trouble is, parents always think that the way they do things is the only way. I'd like to be tidier, but I just never seem to get it together. I sometimes think they only have kids so that they can push them around.

Dirty Genes

I've always thought that there's a strong case for suggesting that whether you're tidy or not is genetically programmed. In other words, it might not actually be your fault. This could explain why some people are perfectly happy living in chaos and getting messier and messier, while others could live in a pigsty for a week and come out, not only looking immaculate, but smelling of freshly bathed babies.

True Story

I once walked into someone's flat that was so chaotic

I was convinced she'd been burgled: drawers pulled open, old magazines all over the floor – and a sadly neglected Hoover, covered in dust, sitting sulkily in the corner. 'Oh this is nothing,' she cried cheerfully when I commented on it. 'I tidied up this morning.'

(Moral: one man's tidy, is another man's chaos.)

How to Handle Your Parents

1. You aren't going to like this, but the best advice is to compromise (a bit!). If you think you're due for a parental inspection or invasion, whip round the room making it slightly less disgusting. Pick up the obvious things from the floor, and remember that no one will

notice how overstuffed your wardrobe is if you keep the door shut. Finally, don't forget to scrape that horrid green mould out of the old coffee mugs.

2. Tell them you know it's a mess, but you want to finish some homework first (this might buy you some time, but not a lot!).

3. Shock them. Just once in a while, *before they ask*, do something completely out of the usual – like Hoovering or something, or . . . dare I even whisper the words 'washing' and 'up' in the same sentence? It will rock them out of their foregone conclusions, for sure. The trade-off is often awesome, especially if you want a favour back, like being allowed to stay out an extra hour. And a good impression could stave off the nagging for weeks. Be warned, though, that if you're tidy anyway, the only thing they'll notice is if you let your standards drop. Where did being good ever get the brother of the Prodigal Son, I ask? (See the Bible.)

4. Find out some names of famous, successful people who were notoriously untidy – like Quentin Crisp (writer) or George W. Bush (American president). Better still, choose someone they really admire, and say you've been learning about them at school – that'll cut 'em off at the pass. If you can't think of any real people, make them up.

5. This is a big one. Try to convince the oldies that worrying about things that don't actually affect them (like the state of your room) is wasting their twilight years. By putting the responsibility back on you, it will not only make their lives much easier, but, if it all goes pear-shaped, and you do die from some terrible disease (like that one you can get in hospitals), they needn't blame themselves.

Getting Organised

From someone who wasn't very, let me extol the virtues of being organised. I assure you, the time you save by not having to try and find things all the time, is far outweighed by the time it takes to keep things tidy and organised. Also, bear in mind that it is actually just as easy to arrive on time as to be continually late. Try setting your watch ten minutes early – it really works.

And Finally . . .

Remember, someone once said that cleanliness is next to godliness. I don't know how they worked that one out. I thought God was supposed to have made everything . . . surely that must include dirt!

CHAPTER THREE

You Are What You Wear (or Are You?)

Isn't it amazing? It's as if your parents think they have a one-way right to have a go at the way you look. Imagine what they'd say if you did it back to them. Have you ever wanted to have a conversation like this?

Daughter: Mum, PLEEEASE, you're not really going to wear that, are you? What if anyone sees you?

Mother: I've no idea what you mean. Anyway, I thought I might try a slightly younger look.

Daughter: I so don't think so, Mum! It looks as if you're trying a bit too hard.

Mother: I'd have thought you'd like it, you wear things like this yourself. *(I promise you, if you and your parents do dress in the same way, something's gone very wrong somewhere.)*

Daughter: Yeah, but I'm fourteen!

Mother: I think it makes me look younger.

Daughter: Well, just don't talk to me if you see me in the street.

Warning!

I severely recommend that you don't ever talk to your parents like this (even if you sometimes might want to). If you do, you'll be booking into a foster home quicker than you can even say 'double-standard'. Unfortunately, the truth is that these sorts of arguments don't work the other way round.

Ever since time began, parents have had something to say, nearly always critical, about what their children choose to wear. It's as if at any one time there's this standard to which everyone must conform and to move away from it is a sin similar to gross indecency. Here's the sort of conversation you might expect:

Father: Isn't it about time you got that hair cut? You look like a hippie.

Son: C'mon, Dad. There's no such thing as hippies any more.

Father: I even liked it better when it was all sticking up all over the place and covered in that gel stuff.

Son: Sorry, Dad. That's all a bit last week. I'm into the surfer look now.

Father: How appropriate – seeing as we live just about as far as we can from the sea.

Son: Have you finished? I was rather hoping to go out in the next few days. *(Nice one – but be very careful, being cheeky can sometimes take the heat out of things, but it can also backfire. As a rule, the old folk don't like being answered back.)*

Father: That's enough of that. Anyway you can't be thinking of going out dressed like that, you'll frighten all the animals and children – or should that be fish, now you're a surfer?

Son (ignoring joke):   Right, I'll be off then.

Father: And do those ridiculous plimsolls up *(a quaint, old-fashioned term for trainers)* – you'd think with the amount they cost, you'd wear them properly.

Son: Dad! Please keep up. Nobody does their laces up these days.

Father: Well, don't come running to us if you break your neck, that's all.

Son: Wouldn't I find that a bit difficult?

Parent's View

I just can't work out what he imagines he looks like. You work your bits off to provide a nice place for him to live and give him all the things you never had and he ends up looking like he lives in a cardboard box. We give him extra money for clothes at Christmas and birthdays, yet he manages to end up in the filthiest, scruffiest rags he can find. God knows what the neighbours must think. I'm surprised we don't get social services round, accusing us of neglect. And doesn't he have any sense of self-respect? He's letting himself down, as much as the rest of us. Please God, let this be just a phase.

Teenager's View

Poor old Dad. He'd have me dressed like one of those blokes that does the weather – with hair looking like it gets taken off at night. Talking of hair, just because his front and back bald patches are on a mission to meet in the middle, he seems to want to take it out on me – he's just jealous. Next, he'll be pulling the strands across the bald bit, hoping nobody will notice. One day I'm going to shave all my hair off and run down Chestnut Avenue, stark naked. That'll *really* give him and the neighbours something to talk about.

And why do they keep going on about it being just

a phase? If I hear them saying that one more time, they'll be blood on their ever-so-tasteful carpets. Do they really think that one day, out of the blue, I'm going to come downstairs wearing the sort of gear they wear? I *so* don't think so. I reckon I'm always going to dress like this, so they'll have to get used to it. And if I change my mind, it'll be because *I* want to.

Nothing Lasts For Ever

Beware! What we think looks pretty cool one year, can be as naff as ninepence the next. You might well think that piercings and tattoos will be around for ever, but you can bet your mum and dad's Lonnie Donegan albums that they won't. Parents and their kids are often as guilty as each other of missing the point. You get uptight when they have a go at what you're wearing, but wet yourself when you see pictures of them when they were young. The more they say that *everyone* was into that stuff in those days, the more ridiculous it seems. And you can bet your own life that your kids (if you ever have any) will roll about on the carpets (if you have any) when you get out the dusty old family album in years to come. Fashion to young people is about NOW – not some time in the distant past, or even in the future.

So What Is Fashion?

Completely daft! That's what fashion is – and it always has been. No wonder it's so difficult to see eye to eye on the subject. The trouble is, fashion is part of what holds modern society together. Clothes, make-up and hairstyles are the only way us boring humans can show at first glance to those around us who we are, or who we'd like to be (or who we'd like not to be).

Most home-grown fashion trends these days come from the street, and are set by ordinary people in their teens or mid-twenties. It used to be different. Way back in the fifties and sixties, magazine editors in London used to wait with bated breath to see what nonsense the Paris designers were going to come up with, and then pass it on to their eager public. Now it's the opposite – since the birth of the trendsetting British teenager, the French designers wait with bated breath to see what people like you and your mates are going to do next and then copy it. They often end up with silly overblown versions, carrying ludicrous price tags, in some up-its-own-bottom magazine like *Vogue* or *Harper's Bazaar*.

The celebrated fashion designer Vivienne Westwood has been credited with giving rather painful birth to the punk fashion movement of the late seventies and eighties. (You must have seen pictures of them, featuring ripped clothes held together with safety pins, spiky multi-coloured hair and metal studs through just about every bit of their bodies.) Well, *oh no* she didn't. She, like many others before her and since, simply looked out of the window and clocked what was going on outside. She then cleverly adapted it, named it 'punk rock', and flogged her own version for squillions down the King's Road in Chelsea. And who bought it? All the people who couldn't come up with the look for themselves, of course.

Long ago, major retail outfits and department stores cottoned on to the fact that the less imaginative teenagers always seem to copy the way-out ones. By cloning this look and watering it down so that mummies and daddies might find it a little more acceptable, they reach a huge market of trend followers. Mind you, it cannot be denied that by the time one of these new trends is in the major stores and available to kids and grannies alike, it's usually as fresh as last month's kippers to the people who invented it.

Non-Fashion Victims

Most of the time we try to look like our mates and, if we can afford it and as far as possible, like our heroes. Maybe we think their style and talent will rub off. However, you might have noticed that there are some youngsters who never seem to be influenced by youth culture. All they seem to want to do is grow up to look like their parents – the fourteen-going-on-forty style.

For years the offspring of the royals have adhered to this sad way of carrying on, but recently there are signs that the latest litter appear to be breaking out. Rumour has it, however, the oldies don't really approve. Surprise, surprise!

But why do some teenagers want to emulate their parents? Maybe these youngsters think that if their parents and their associates have done so well looking like they do, why knock it? Maybe they even think it helps, and that people will take them more seriously, and treat them more seriously, if they're all suited up. Not everyone, but some people – the *right* people . . . right?

Leaders of the Pack

To explain the need to look totally unique is far more difficult. Some of the most outrageously dressed people I know come from totally ordinary homes with totally straight parents. I can quite see, however, that if you were brought up by Mr and Mrs Normal of Normal Crescent, Normalton-on-Sea, you might be good and ready to break out, for fear of becoming too normal (i.e. dull) yourself.

We all like to think of ourselves as being where it's at fashion-wise, but very few of us want to really stand out in a crowd. There are probably one or two people at your school, however, who don't think like that. They might be the sort of people who love showing off – and are prepared to take all the reaction – good or bad – which inevitably comes with it. As long as they are noticed, that's all that matters. These people will probably regard themselves as fashion leaders and will take the mickey out of anyone who goes with the flow. But they must be so careful, for individuals who take it that far can so easily turn into fashion *victims*. Fashion and your appearance should only be a part of your life – there's no way it can express everything about you. This is something that has happened to every generation, right back to when people first started wearing clothes. If your parents try to tell you they weren't like you in their day, chances are they are not being completely truthful or have forgotten.

How to Get Round the Old Fogies

1. If you've got any friends whose appearance is less acceptable than yours, take them home to meet your parents. It might take the pressure off you a bit.
2. Never get into dressing in a way that upsets your parents just for the sake of it. We know it's their problem, but why rub their noses in it?
3. Try to convince them that the way you look doesn't actually affect *their* everyday lives. If you dress outrageously for school, however, then it's you who must be prepared to take whatever's handed out to you, and not go home whimpering to Mummy and Daddy. Personal responsibility is what the whole clothes issue is about. Come to that, that's what being a teenager's all about!

4. If they say you look a mess, tell them it's because you've grown out of all your clothes and are really upset because you've nothing to wear. You can make a great sob story out of this. The trouble with this approach is that if they do fund the operation, chances are they'll want a say in what you buy.

5. If you are a girl and want to wear your skirt shorter than the current regulation length, you could wear something in a stretch material which can go up and down according to how you feel. This is particularly relevant at school, which can be a constant battle for the fashion-conscious young person.

Another Warning!

Just bear in mind the fickle nature of fashion – regardless of however much it divides you and your parents. Tattoos, nose rings, lip rings, eyebrow studs, etc. are things that you might want to think about seriously before making a decision. They might seem dead cool now, but in a few years' time, fashions will have changed and you'll be stuck with them, like a zebra with its stripes. Are you happy with that idea?

Remember that if you wear a nose ring for a long time, the hole it leaves can resemble a third nostril halfway up your nose. Other piercings can close up, but will still leave a mark. Tattoos can be removed, but it's horribly expensive and the scar that may be left behind could be more noticeable than what you were trying to get rid of. The only way to really get rid of a tattoo is to remove the offending limb. Let's just hope it's not on your head or face.

If you want to adorn your body, by all means go for it, but consider things that aren't permanent. I mean, what do *you* think of older people with tattoos?

CHAPTER FOUR

Call That Music?

Every generation thinks their parents' music is old-fashioned – and parents think that their children's taste is too modern. Can you imagine your dad bursting into your room and asking if you could turn the volume up a bit because he really likes it? I think not. Whatever you're currently into, you can bet that your ma and pa won't be. But, as annoying as the arguments can be, if you think about it, maybe that's the way it *should* be. After all, pop music reflects the concerns of the people who are listening to it – and we all know how much these concerns change over the years. Maybe it's really important that you have a style of music that your parents *don't* understand. Who knows, maybe that's the *point* of pop music (and teenagers!). Ever had a row like this at home?

Father (practically smashing the door off its hinges): Can
you turn that racket down? We can't hear

EastEnders and the dog's started howling!

Teenager: What? Sorry, Dad, I can't hear you.

Father: I said, turn it down.

Teenager: It's only on level five.

Father: Is level six when the roof caves in and your ears begin to bleed?

Teenager: It's meant to be played loud.

Father: Why? There's not even a tune – it sounds like people jumping up and down on a van roof – with me inside.

Teenager: It's better than all that boring stuff you put on.

Father: We don't inflict it on you though, do we? Half the street has to listen to you.

Teenager: You're right. We should charge them money.

Parent's View

Kids today! Just because we think their music's tuneless drivel, they think we don't understand what good music is. How arrogant is that? Anyway, what's there to understand with the music they like? A bunch of loud, ignorant yobs prancing around in too-big (or too-tight) clothes, droning on and on about something or other. What's it called . . . R'n'B, garage, rap, hip-hop . . . I don't know what. And another thing, why can't kids today listen to something at a volume that doesn't blow the windows out?

Teenager's View

I hope I never get like them. They seem to think that anything I play must be terrible. Is it because they don't respect my opinion or do they just think that the whole development of popular music ended when they were young?

Actually, I don't give a monkey's whether they like my stuff or not – I just wish they wouldn't go on about it. And why do they get so arsey when I say I don't like theirs?

A New Generation

Teenage rebellion, as we think of it, wasn't really invented till the late fifties. Kids like me, born towards the end of the Second World War, grew up, for the first time ever, not wanting to be like their parents. They didn't want to look like them, talk like them, and certainly didn't want to tune into the sort of boring old stuff they'd been listening to. To be fair, it wasn't necessarily the fact that their parents were deliberately being dull and oppressive. They'd just come out of a long, horrid war and were trying to get some sort of a life together while coping with rationing and the remaining effects of the economic depression of the thirties.

The first teenage rebellion would have come as quite

a shock to the parents who were probably the last generation who had always done what their parents had told them (and believed they were right!).

The Birth of Rock and Roll

Rock and roll hit England like a tidal wave. It was the upbeat wild child of an affair between grumpy deep South blues and somewhat tedious but often jolly country and western music. The American performer Bill Haley (a rather chubby man with a shiny suit and a shinier hairdo) led a band called the Comets. In 1955, when their first single, the now legendary 'Rock Around the Clock', managed to get played on the radio, literally everyone under eighteen, apart from swots and choirboys, went crazy, much to the distress of their parents and the Establishment. There were even questions asked in parliament about whether it should be banned. If anything, this only strengthened the teenage movement. At last there was a form of music which was all theirs and they weren't about to let it go.

It was like opening a floodgate. Soon, a whole stream of fabulous records were pouring into the country, from living legends like Elvis Presley and Buddy Holly, and slightly later Little Richard and Aretha Franklin. In Britain, rather pale imitations, like the lamentable Cliff Richard, Marty Wilde and Billy Fury, tried their best to cash in on what had been labelled the 'Devil's music' but one by one they fell away and Cliff – realising the game was up – joined the other side (God). One of the only British groups to catch the spirit of this new music was led by a young man called Lonnie Donegan. This raw, rhythmic sound was called skiffle and although it only had a relatively short shelf-life, it didn't matter – teenagers at last had a sound and a look of their own and everything that went before it went straight into Room 101.

When Will They Ever Learn?

The trouble with a 'new thing', is that it eventually becomes 'a not new thing', and the trouble for a lot of people who really went for the 'new thing' is that they fell into exactly the same trap as the generation they had ridiculed. When the rock and rolling teenagers grew up and became parents themselves in the seventies and eighties, they couldn't understand why their kids didn't think their music was the greatest thing ever. And so the pattern was set.

As every new musical trend passes out of fashion, it leaves casualties in its wake. That's what your parents are now. But they still think they know best and they'll probably be buying all those naff 'Best Of' collections on CD you see advertised on telly.

This is all rather a long way of saying that the battle between parents and their teenagers over music and how loudly it's played – just as with fashion and how clothes are worn – will run as long as parents still think the way they do things is best.

How to Handle Your Parents

1. Use headphones. You can get them now without wires attached, which means you can leap round your room like a mad thing, without anyone being any the wiser. A cool Chrissy present, methinks.
2. Take a peek into their record collection. Amongst all

the Dire Straits, Fleetwood Mac, Eric Clapton and Sade there just *might* be some gems that have had big revivals. People like Jimi Hendrix and even ABBA (though only God and the Swedes know why), or some of the old stuff that might have been covered or sampled by artists you actually quite like. Here's a tip. If you start making nice noises about some of the music they like, you may be surprised at their reaction to yours.

3. If there's absolutely nothing good to say about their music, the best thing you can do is to take your stuff round to a friend's house and let *their* parents do the putting up with it.

A Final Thought . . .

Good music can stand the test of time, but all the other stuff that goes out of date becomes just quaint reminders of a past generation. That's the difference between Cliff Richard and David Bowie.

CHAPTER FIVE

Up All Hours
(How to Stay Out Longer)

The one thing guaranteed to send Ma and Pa to the funny farm fast is any conversation about the prospect of you going out for – and then coming back from – a night of sex, drugs and rock and roll. The truth is that most parents are capable of imagining a much wider range of lurid catastrophes that might befall you than you are yourself. Very often parents remember what tearaways they were when they were young, but cannot bear the idea of their kids even thinking about doing the same.

This is not a new area of dispute. I bet Mr and Mrs Hitler went through it when young Adolf was down at the youth club, and I daresay even Mary and Joseph (what was their surname?) used to sit up at night worrying about their precious Jesus – and we all know what a goody-goody *He* turned out to be.

What it boils down to is trust. Explain to your parents that it looks like they don't trust you to make the decisions that *they* made (or maybe didn't make) to prevent themselves sliding down the slippery slope to hell and damnation. Try to convince them otherwise – or better still, show them. It might not always work, but at least you'll have tried.

Girl Guidance

Girls often get a worse time of it than boys when it comes to parents watching their every move. This is probably because parents believe that boys are specifically designed to lead girls astray. They also tend to believe that boys are less at risk themselves – when studies show that violence among males is more common. It has always been easier for boys to be drawn into it than girls – even if they don't want to be. When my kids were teenagers, my son and his friends were far more likely to be picked on late at night than my daughter and hers.

But the risks of violence, pregnancy and STIs, alcohol and drug abuse are real, and it pays to be aware – and a little forgiving of your parents' concerns. Despite what often appears to be gross interference in your life, just remember, they aren't doing for their health.

Here's a typical conversation you might have on the subject of parental control:

Girl: Dad, what time do I have to be in tonight? *(Girls often ask their fathers first – dads are generally a softer touch.)*

Father: Not too late, darling, but you'd better ask your mother to get the exact time. *(A typical male buck-passing trick. Dads might actually worry more about their daughters, because they know what boys are like, but seldom want to appear to be spoilsports.)*

Girl: Mum, is it all right if I stay at the party till twelve? That's the time all my friends have been told, and Dad didn't seem to mind. *(That's two little porkies in one: 1) that everyone else's parents are more easygoing and 2) that the other parent has already given in.)*

Mother: No. You know the rules. I'd like you back by eleven. That's quite late enough. *(Late enough for what? you might ask.)*

Girl: Oh, Mum, you know that's daft. I'll seem like a right twit having to come home before every one else. Do I *have* to leave at eleven?

Mother: You're *not* leaving at eleven. That's the time I want you back here.

40

Girl: But there won't be time for anything if I leave that early.

Mother: Exactly. What do you want to do that requires another hour?

Girl: How will I know till I'm there? Look, it's a party. Anyway, I'll have my phone.

Mother: What sort of a party is it?

Girl: Oh, you know – pass-the-parcel, jelly and ice cream, balloons outside the front door – oh yes and Coco the Clown's coming at . . . *(Beware of sarcasm. It seldom works.)*

Mother: Don't get clever with me, my girl. I've told you the rules.

Girl: Oh, Mum. Pleeeeease! *(This is not going well. Pleading seldom works either. It implies that you've run out of good reasons to defend your position.)*

Mother: No, and that's my final word.

Girl: But why?

Mother: Because I say so. *(This is generally the end of most of these kinds of conversations. 'Because I say so' are the most commonly used words by parents to end any dispute with their teenagers.)*

Parent's View

God, who'd have ever thought I'd have heard myself

saying those words. I remember how mad it used to make me when my mum and dad said it. I could have throttled them.

But this is different. Doesn't she realise that I'm only doing it for her own protection? It makes me remember all the bad paths that I could have gone down but luckily didn't. Whenever I got myself into compromising situations, I just used to imagine my parents' faces when I ended up in trouble and needed their help – that was enough to stop me in my tracks. But my daughter clearly doesn't think like that.

Worst of all, boys will be there and we all know what they're after – one thing. I can still remember them at school on Monday mornings, giggling about how far they got with various girls at the weekend. Just look at her father. He tried to get me into bed on our second date when his parents went away for the weekend. They're all the same. Well, they're not going to have their way with my daughter. And I don't want her wandering the streets at all hours. It's far too dangerous. And what if she got driven home by some boy who has drunk himself silly – or she could be getting drunk herself . . . not to mention taking drugs . . . I'll never be able to get to sleep until she's home safely . . .

Anyway, if we didn't lay down rules, she'd stay out

all night, and she'd be so exhausted she'd be no good for school or anything.

Teenager's View

Talk about missing the point. You'd think, talking to those two, that parties were like assault courses, where you'd be lucky to get out in one piece. What's so special about eleven o'clock, anyway? I feel like Cinder-bloody-ella. The only difference is that Mum thinks that instead of turning into a flipping pumpkin, or whatever, I'm going to drop my knickers on the stroke of eleven. Either that, or transmute into a drug-crazed, drop-out fiend. They're bonkers. If I really wanted to get laid, or drink myself into a coma, or hit the long and winding white powder trail, I could do it any time of day and with practically anyone (and practically anywhere). Bad things don't only happen after eleven o'clock.

How to Handle Your Parents

Have you ever been fishing? Probably not. If you've ever watched an experienced fisherman bringing in a catch, you'll notice he doesn't rush to yank it out of the water. The secret is to play it really slowly and gently, so that it doesn't think it's being caught. Then you ease it towards the shore and, hey presto!

What's fishing got to do with you? Well, it's the same with parents. If you take it nice and easy, you'll be surprised at what you can achieve. So . . .

1. The first couple of times you want to stay out really late . . . don't! Act the dutiful daughter (or son). When the oldsters tell you a time to come home, stick to it right to the second. Bear with me, there's method in this madness.

2. If they're still up when you get in, instead of going straight to bed, volunteer little bits of information about the evening – nothing to worry them, of course, just who you spoke to and what the venue was like. Avoid any references to cigarettes and alcohol, etc. If there's nothing you could remotely talk about, make it up. The more they think they know, the more secure they'll feel. Bless 'em. Also, if they see that your interests don't lie in drugs, sex and alcohol and that you have a good sense of judgement, you'll gain their trust.

3. Before the event, introduce them to some of the people you're going with to reassure them that you will have people who will be looking out for you. Choose

the most sensible, normal-looking friends if you can (no tattoos or face piercings) – you can always ditch them later.

4. If you plan to look really outrageous or sexy, change your clothes when you're out of the house (see **Chapter Three: You Are What You Wear**). If you look *too* provocative, it'll only make them worry more. Taking a jumper is ideal here – not only will you get less of a hard time from your parents, it's a good way of getting less of the wrong sort of attention at night in the streets.

CINDERELLA GOT TO STAY OUT TILL MIDNIGHT!

ALTERNATIVE 'PARTY BAG' FILLED WITH COOL CLOTHES ETC.

PARTY BAG

5. Arrange how you're getting home ahead of time – both for safety's sake and to reassure your parents that you won't be wandering the streets alone. The best thing is to hang out in groups. A bit of discussion

earlier could save you a lot of angst. This is something you could try to communicate to your parents. If they really believe you are not into sex, drugs and booze and are simply interested in having a good time, you'll probably gain their trust.

If you do all these things a few times, there's a fair chance your parents might begin to think you know what you're doing and not believe you'll be mainlining crack next week or that they'll be welcoming grandchildren before the year's out. They might even relax their rules and eventually let you stay out longer. The secret of dealing with parents over the issue of staying out late is to make them feel that you are totally in control and that they can depend on your good judgement. Never give them the impression that you are floating around wondering what you are going to try next. Have fun – but know your limitations. It's a trust thing, after all.

CHAPTER SIX

Who's Responsible?
(You, Your Parents and the Law)

It's a bit weird. Parents as a rule seem to confuse their role in their teenager's life. They encourage them through all their early changes, from crawling to walking, gurgling to speaking and even peeing and pooing from nappy to potty. But when the apple of their eye turns into a teenager all that seems to go out of the window. Their supportive, understanding approach disappears despite the fact that you're probably going through even more drastic (at least, that's how it seems) mental and physical changes, which can cause you to be totally out of control of your day-to-day emotions. Could one of the reasons be that they are judging you by their own criteria? It's as if you've become a fully fledged adult overnight. Most parents have a problem realising that you are growing up and need to make your own judgements about stuff.

Does this sound familiar?:

Mother: Didn't you hear me? I asked you to put the plates in the dishwasher.

Son: Ugh!

Mother: Look, it's not as if I ask you to do much. I can't even seem to talk to you these days. I'm not going to bother in future.

Son (under breath): That's the first good news I've heard today.

Mother: Why can't you be nice for a change?

Son: Why can't you get off my case for a change?

Mother: When you do do anything, it's with such bad grace.

Son: Look, I'll do the bloody dishes, OK? Just not right now. Five minutes isn't going to make a great difference.

Mother: If I added up all the five minutes you waste . . .

Son: You'd have wasted even more time!

You can annoy your parents by doing something other than what they want you to do, but you can also seriously hack them off by doing nothing at all . . .

Mother: It's eleven o'clock. How long are you going to stay in bed? Are you going into hibernation or something?

Teenager: Most animals are allowed to hibernate for months.

Mother: How can you lie in bed on such a lovely day?

Teenager: But I *am* having a lovely day. It just doesn't involve being vertical.

Mother: That's not the point. Bed is for night-time. If you went to bed earlier, you wouldn't need to sleep all day.

Teenager: Why can't I do what I want? It is the weekend. It's bad enough having to get up in the middle of the night for school.

Parent's View

When I was her age, I had to get up and help my parents around the house. If we ask *her* to do anything, she turns her nose up at us. And she wouldn't agree with us about anything even if she knew we were right. This generation think they can carry on just as they please.

Teenager's View

This is worse than being in prison. I'll bet the warders don't come round rattling your bars to wake you up every five minutes. Why do parents think that the way they live is written in tablets of stone for all future generations to follow? If it's not one thing it's another. Eat when we eat and eat *what* we eat. Sleep when we sleep and get up when we get up. Like what we like and dislike what we dislike . . . It goes on and on (and on). I bet if I did manage to run away, they'll even disapprove of where I run away to. It's so not fair.

Who Owns You?

When you consider how many times you get things wrong in your parents' eyes, you must wonder if there was a mix-up in the handing-out-the-baby-department in hospital all those years ago. Perhaps you aren't their kid after all. Maybe, somewhere in the world, there are a couple of really cool, laid-back parents who are wishing *their* kid wasn't such a goody-goody. Just think: they could have been your mum and dad.

Your parents have a responsibility to protect you. However, by sticking their noses into just about every corner of your life, even though it might be for the best possible reasons, the result is often counter-productive. You might just decide to ignore their advice, or in fact do the exact opposite, on principle which doesn't help you to form your own judgements, learn from your mistakes, decide what you think or anything constructive.

In any case, young people must be allowed to cock things up for themselves every now and again. People often learn by trial and error in this life (as the headless lion-tamer once tried to say).

Advice Centre

1. If your parents are hassling you about sleeping in, try to have a discussion with them about what harm sleeping in can really do. You could try pointing out that you get up early for school every weekday. If there are any chores that need to be done, talk about them the day before. Most importantly, work out whether it's worth all the arguing, or whether a compromise might save a load of grief.

2. Point out the things that you *do* handle responsibly – even if it's down to feeding the hamster (if it's still alive) or helping the old lady down the road with her shopping. If there aren't any, simply point out the temptations you manage to resist. If there aren't any of these, then I suggest you stop reading now. You're a hopeless case!

3. Suggest to your parents that telling you what to do and how you must do it all the time actually works against you becoming a responsible adult because you don't get a chance to think for yourself. Get them to tell you simply what they want done and then ask them to let you do it in your own time. This requires having some initiative on your part, but you'll be surprised how much better life will be if

you grab a bit of responsibility for yourself.

4. Tell them as gently as possible that, although you're grateful for all they do for you, they need to help you gain your independence from them as you grow older. If that doesn't work, tell them you think there really was a mix-up at the hospital and you're going out to look for your real parents.

A Final Thought . . .

A lady called Margaret Turnbull once said, 'No man is responsible for his father.' Unfortunately, it doesn't work the other way round.

CHAPTER SEVEN

Money — the Root of All Evil
(Who Needs It?)

Money is one of life's crucial subjects that seems to intrude into every aspect of our lives (and nearly every argument).

One of the things that you can be almost certain of in life – apart from death and inedible school dinners – is that however much money you've got, it will never be quite enough. Take a look at the very rich people on those reality programmes on the telly. They all seem to be looking around greedily for their next million. One of the problems with having loads of money (not that I've ever experienced it) is that there's always going to be someone with just that bit more than you and they're bound to make you want a bit more too.

It's nice to think that your parents don't want you to be

short of the things you really need. Therein lies the problem. What you think you really need and what they think you really need are generally two completely different things. Unless you've got parents with so much money they don't care who spends it or how, this problem won't ever get resolved. However much they give, it will not be nearly enough for you but will be far too much for them. It's a fact of life, like spots and grumpy teachers.

Money gets parents' knickers in a twist just thinking about it:

Teenager: Any chance of borrowing a couple of quid till next week? We're all going out this evening and I've run out.

Parent: How is that? You only had your pocket money a couple of days ago. I really can't think what you spend it on.

Teenager: So why are you always going on about your housekeeping money disappearing?

Parent: That's different. I don't spend any of that money on myself. I can't even think of the last time I . . . *(There usually follows a long list of things that they reckon they're deprived of.)*

Teenager: Oh, come on, Ma! You and Dad spend more on a round of drinks in the pub than I get a

	month. I bet you can't remember what it's like being really broke.
Parent:	Broke? You don't know the meaning of the word. When I was young, we had to beg for pocket money, and when we did get it, there was no coming back for more. We used to dream of . . . *(Oh no! You've just gone and opened a can of worms and it will go on until you both die of exhaustion.)*
Teenager:	Anyway, I can't see how getting through a few pounds a week could exactly be called uncontrolled spending.

This sort of conversation leads most parents to believe that you think money grows on trees, and that because you haven't actually had to work for it yourself, it has no value. Not only that, but they seem to insist that whatever money you have should be spent on sensible things – as if they never treat themselves to life's luxuries.

But just think how quickly you get through your pocket money, or Christmas money or any other cash that might come your way. Well, multiply this by goodness-knows-what and you might begin to realise how much it costs to run a family like yours (unless you live in a hole in the ground and eat worms). Who pays for it all? Your mum and dad of course.

But why shouldn't they, you might ask? After all, you didn't beg them to produce you all those years ago. But, just before you swear at your parents the next time they turn down your request for a ninety-quid pair of trainers, or tell you to go easy on the house phone calls to friends that you could almost shout to out of the bedroom window, make sure that it really is meanness that's driving them and not that they are struggling financially. If they're not, count yourself lucky.

Everything you see in the house, right down to the last Coco Pop and sheet of loo paper has to be bought by them, and the things that you *really* need – food, heat, clothes (and the last sheet of loo paper) seldom go down in price. A family is like an ever-widening mouth: the more you shove down it, the more it wants, and every month, as night follows day, the family budget grows, and disappears (like a bucket with a hole) faster than the amount of money that's put in it.

Here's another conversation that might seem familiar . . .

Mother: Are those rings new? I've never seen them before.

Daughter: I've had them weeks. Do you like them?

Mother: I thought you said that you'd run out of money for your school lunches.

Daughter: I have. I told you, I bought these weeks ago.

Mother: When are you going to learn to budget your pocket money? When I was your age I only got a fraction of what you get now, and I always managed.

Daughter: Yes, but things cost so much less in the olden days. You're always telling me how much things keep going up. They were really cheap, anyway. They came from that stall in the market.

Mother: That doesn't matter. Buying them still meant you didn't have enough money for the things you need. I don't have money to waste.

Daughter: I always thought my money was mine to do with as I liked.

Mother: Look, my girl, when you earn your own money, you can spend it how you like.

Daughter: One day, I'll hold you to that. Anyway, I bought them with the last of my birthday money.

Parent's View

Honestly, they think that just because inflation means that everything costs more than it used to, we had oodles more cash to throw about when we were young. It wouldn't have occurred to me to splash out on a silly set of rings – however 'cheap' they were – if it meant I couldn't have afforded to pay for my own lunch. Not that she's ever known what it's like to run out of money completely . . .

Teenager's View

Only last week Mum asked me if I bought drugs with my pocket money. Who's she kidding? I nearly said that unless they start selling weed at car boot sales or charity shops, there'd be a severe chance my meagre pittance of an allowance wouldn't even run to the papers to roll it up in. That joke would go down like a ton of bricks, of course. I wonder what they'd say if I started to give them advice on what they spend their money on?

How to Get What You Want Without Upsetting the Old Folk

1. Show your parents you have an awareness of the value of money by not asking them for every new must-have that you fancy. Maybe grit your teeth and go shopping with them to show that you understand how much it costs to run a household.

2. Sit down with your parents and discuss – with an open mind! – how much you think you should be

getting and why. Agree that birthday and Christmas money can go towards what you want, and work out with them how much of your pocket money should be spent on essentials and if you could have a clothing allowance perhaps, then negotiate how much you can have on top of that. Listen to their point of view and try and reach a compromise. If this doesn't go as well as you'd hoped, you can always console yourself with the fact you won't have to answer to them forever!

3. Without robbing banks, try to get hold of your own money. If you can crack making the loot now, just think how easy it will be when you have to do it for a living. It's not easy, I admit. Saturday jobs are thin on

the ground and they can often seem to be little more than slave labour. There are, however, a million other things you can do, such as dog-walking, babysitting, car washing and lawnmowing. If there is anything that someone with more money than you can't be bothered to do, you're in with a chance – even in your own home. Use your imagination. There are also certain activities that your parents hate doing – household tasks like cleaning the oven, feeding the cat, Hoovering the stairs (or the dog) – you name it. Plus, having cash that you actually worked for yourself gives you a real buzz.

4. If you do manage to earn your own money, your parents will have even less right to tell you what to do with it. If you want to blow the lot on daft T-shirts or text messaging Mars, it's your affair, unless it's something that could harm you physically (like buying a gun or a lion), which they'd be within their rights to speak up against.

5. If you want to be really licky, buy your parents a little present with your first payment. It's sensational PR and, with a bit of luck, it'll make them feel guilty about their mean behaviour in the past. Don't fret, you'll never have to do it again – the shock of the experience will probably keep them in order for ages.

6. If you become aware of your mum and dad cutting back and having a bit of a rough time financially, try and trim your demands accordingly, and let them know that you've clocked what they're going through. When things get easier, there's a fair chance they'll remember the consideration you showed them.

CHAPTER EIGHT

The Bad Things in Life
(Smoking, Drinking and Taking Drugs)

Fasten your seatbelts, we are now about to enter deepest Doublestandardland. Although your parents might deny it, they must have known the dangers from smoking, drinking and taking drugs – it's just that these days the warnings are much more in-your-face. OK, they want you to be better informed, but it's probably more that they don't want you to go near any mistakes they might have made. That's all very well, of course, but the trouble is, anything your parents tell you about those three Bad Things in Life will no doubt sound like a huge dollop of 'Do as I say, not as I did'.

Not that we know everything there is to know these days – nor can we more easily believe what the average person tells us. A lot of the stuff that goes round the clubs and pubs is of highly dubious origin. If cocaine, for instance, isn't bad enough, it can be cut (mixed) with anything from baking powder to lavatory cleaner to bulk up the volume. And marijuana can be 'laced' with something harder, such as crack cocaine, without you knowing it until it's too late. There are more studies than you can count these days, telling us of the varying long-term effects of drugs, so much so that you can never be quite sure what could happen. Nor can your parents, so it's good to talk over the subject with them, That way, they might just begin to trust you on the subject.

Whilst some people will use drugs and get away with it, others might not be quite so lucky. And some effects might not show up until much later, sometimes years later. Reports are perpetually coming out with new evidence and findings with regard to drugs and their physiological and psychological effects. There has been a lot in the papers recently about the link between marijuana use and mental illness, for example. You might think you have got away with taking drugs at the time, but you could turn into Mr or Miss Fuzzybrain when you're older, or Mr or Miss No-Brain-at-All.

Cigarettes

If your parents find out you've been having the odd cig-gie, the inevitable confrontation could well go some-thing like this:

Father: And just how long have you been smoking?

Son: Who, me? I don't know what you mean.

Father: Ah, I see. Someone must have borrowed your mouth to smoke with. Your breath stinks of tobacco.

Son: Oh yeah, I remember, I did try a cigarette recently.

Father: Are you crazy? You must be deaf and blind! You can't have missed all the stuff telling you how dangerous it is. It's written on the packets bigger

than the brand name. Everyone knows smoking
kills you.

Son: It hasn't done you much harm. Didn't you used
to smoke?

Father: Yes, but I had the good sense to pack up when I
was in my twenties. *(Three guesses where this is
going . . .)*

Son: Fine. I'll pack it up when I get there, then I'll still
be OK according to you . . . won't I? *(Game, set
and match to you!)*

Parent's View

Why, oh why can't he for once take my word for it? I
just can't seem to get it into his thick skull that smoking
eventually kills you. That'll teach me to admit I once
smoked. I thought it might help him to realise that we
gave up because we realised it was so dangerous for my
health.

Teenager's View

Anyone would think I was on eighty a flipping day the
way he goes on. Honestly, I hardly think a quick fag in
the park shelter on the way home from school is going to
have me in intensive care. Parents seem to lose the plot so
quickly.

It's not just that either. They seem to think that all the major drug syndicates have got a representative outside our school gates. Why can't they just trust me for once? Anybody would think I want to be chain-smoking, drugged-up alcoholic. At this rate, they'll drive me to it.

Do as I Say . . .

Only parents who have never dragged on a cigarette can wave the flag of self-righteousness. But very often, reformed heavy smokers (or drinkers) are the worst naggers – and how unfair is that? Just because they went over the top, doesn't mean their offspring will.

No one really knows why some people get addicted and others don't. There are theories that it could be genetic, in that if either of your parents are smokers or alcoholics then you could be more likely to smoke or become an alcoholic yourself. Or it could be that growing up in such an environment, addictive behaviour can seem normal. But that doesn't necessarily mean that because your parents smoke, you will – it could always have the opposite effect and put you right off!

As for horrid things like lung cancer and emphysema, they only usually only kick in when you're in your late forties or fifties. There's a good chance, therefore, that you wouldn't see your parents suffering until it was too late for you. If your mum and dad smoke, but are determined that you don't, try to understand. You could even feel a bit sorry for them. You can bet it's not because they want to, but more likely that they haven't the will-power to pack it up. Most smokers loathe this expensive addiction and wish they could knock it on the head. According to health experts, nicotine (a chief ingredient in tobacco) is one of the most addictive of all drugs. That's why a parent who smokes, and can't kick the habit, is often more adamant than others that their kids don't start.

The good news is that since 1972 when forty to fifty per cent of adults smoked, the numbers have plummeted. Unfortunately, the bad news is that this isn't true amongst you lot. Despite all the warnings, teenage smoking is on the increase, particularly amongst girls. So, you can see why your parents might seem particularly persistent when it comes to nagging you about the dangers of smoking. The facts are available for everyone to see. Ultimately, it's your choice – and you shouldn't need your parents going on at you to recognise that smoking is bad news for your health.

The Demon Drink

Most of my adult friends have at least one alcoholic drink every single day. If the figures regarding the number of units of alcohol it is safe to consume are to be believed, a lot of them are tottering well over the danger line – and it is well known that alcohol is responsible for more and more health problems and premature deaths all the time. Drinking, unfortunately, has become a big part of British culture and is present at practically every social event – from christenings to weddings and even funerals. Worse still, the amount of alcohol consumed by young people is increasing at an alarming rate, with manufacturers encouraging the phenomenon with the production of alcopops and 'cool', pretty-looking drinks to get them hooked. It would also be fair to say that the example adults are giving you young people leaves a lot to be desired.

Father: Where have you been? I could swear I smelled booze when you came in.

Son: I just had a lager round at Tom's house. That can't be a crime.

Father: I wasn't allowed to drink at your age. Who gave it to you?

Son: Tom's dad. He doesn't seem to have a problem with it.

Father: Next thing we know we'll be having the police bringing you home. I've seen what happens to you youngsters on the television.

Son: I hardly think the police are going to arrest me over half of lager. Anyway, what about you? You often come home from the pub a bit pis– er . . . tiddly.

Parent's View

What's all this binge drinking that the papers are on about? Teenagers always seem to have to do everything to excess. It's different for us – we're experienced. We have a drink most days, but in moderation. We know what we're doing, whereas they don't seem to have a clue these days. All they seem to want to do is see how much they can get down their throats. It beats me where they get the money from to pay for it.

Teenager's View

It's amazing. Every time I have a half of shandy, or a liqueur chocolate at Christmas, I get them breathing down my neck and a lecture on the perils of booze. I reckon they're convinced I'll end up in a cardboard box at Waterloo station. (Mind you, sometimes I think it would be preferable.)

Warning!

Whilst alcohol can be grounds for parents to overreact, their fears are not entirely unfounded. According to data gathered by the Trust for the Study of Adolescence, one in six people who go to the accident and emergency department of hospitals have alcohol-related injuries or problems. After eleven p.m., this number goes up to seven out of ten people!

As fun as alcohol can seem when everyone around you is laughing and drinking, it is also responsible for more and more deaths – alcohol contributes to about half of all cases of people who die younger than they would be expected to.

So enjoy it by all means, but bear the warnings in mind and enjoy it responsibly. If your parents see you are mature in this area, they may even realise that you can be trusted to go out and about where alcohol may be present.

Drugs

There has never been a culture, since monkeys decided to be men, that hasn't swallowed, sniffed or smoked something to make itself jollier. Whether it be dried grass, cactus juice or fermented snakes' dribble, there has always been some substance or other to drag us out of the drudgery of being human. Nowadays the most common drugs are nicotine and alcohol, though many people refuse to acknowledge that they *are* drugs.

But your mum and dad's fears about drugs mostly relate to illegal drugs (e.g. cannabis, speed, ecstasy, LSD, etc.). Many, if not most, parents will have had some contact with some sort of drug or other at some time (whether they acknowledge it or not). The sort of drugs that would have been around during their teenage years would have been much the same as they are now, although ecstasy or its equivalent was only just beginning to appear in the clubs and pubs.

According to a recent report in the *Observer*, the price of all the popular drugs has tumbled over the past few years; some of them have fallen by more than a third. Put another way, in many cities in Britain, a line of cocaine could cost you less than a cappuccino (with or without chocolate on the top). The only good news is that the highest percentage of drug users is no longer in the teenage group. That honour has now shifted to their older brothers and sisters, aged between twenty and twenty-four. A popular myth is that drug use only occurs in run-down inner-city areas and council estates, but figures show that drug abuse is commonplace in more affluent urban areas. Whereas drugs were once perceived as a consolation for the poor and depressed, it seems that many of them (particularly cocaine and ecstasy) have become playthings of the middle classes. So your parents' fears of them being around wherever you go out, may not always be hugely exaggerated. Try to show them that even if you are in a situation where drugs are on offer, you know enough to reject them. It's down to you to convince your parents that you're on the case and are well aware of the pitfalls of drug culture.

Addiction

Could you become addicted to drugs? The short answer is . . . yes. Drugs such as cannabis, or marijuana (grass) are not as physically addictive as others (e.g. crack cocaine, heroin). Scientific studies show that marijuana is less addictive than caffeine and alcohol – and three times less than nicotine. But the great debate tends to be whether use of cannabis leads to taking increasingly stronger things. It has been said that one can become addicted to crack cocaine after only a couple of tries. Bear in mind that different addictions require different levels of exposure, and that people have wildly varying levels of tolerance and addiction to certain substances.

It has been argued that some people's personalities make them more susceptible to addiction. But how do you know if you have an addictive personality? The problem is that, at the age you are now, you probably won't know. As mentioned, we *do* know, however, that it doesn't *necessarily* pass from parent to child, so don't try using them as an excuse. It could be that if either of your parents have an addiction – be it to smoking, alcohol or drugs – using those things might not seem that big a deal to you. It could work the other way, however. Living with a heavy drinker, smoker, or a drug user, could well make you vow never to touch the stuff yourself.

How to Handle Your Parents

1. Realise that, if you smoke, your parents usually won't have to hire a detective to find out. Sooner or later they'll know; so be prepared for confrontation.
2. If your parents have never smoked, your smoking will seem even more of a mystery to them. You don't need them to tell you that nobody actually needs to smoke, so you're instantly on dodgy ground. Think about this for a second. Seeing as the first one you ever try will almost definitely taste crap . . . why persist? Let's

face it, if someone told you that ground-up bat's poo was really a great smoke, even if it tasted foul, and would eventually kill you, you'd tell them to F-off. So what's the difference? Get your head round the idea that, these days, it really is cool *NOT* to smoke. And it's so *not* cool to die in your fifties, coughing up your lungs. Convince your parents (and then yourself) that this is just a phase and that you are already planning to give up.

3. If you have got a real problem with smoking and want to stop, it's probably best to tell them about it. A problem shared is a problem halved.

4. If you're not smoking, but are really worried about your mum and dad's habit, try offering them a deal such as you won't start, if they stop. If it saves their lives (and, more to the point, yours), how bad is that?

5. Avoid, whatever you do, rolling home pissed. It will blow your 'I'm a controlled, sensible person' cover completely (as well as guarantee that you'll feel crap the next morning). If you are a bit sloshed and are expected at home, try to get as much fresh air through your lungs as possible . . . and drink plenty of water. One of the best ways to get sober quickly, by the way, is to walk it off. (Just don't walk on your own at night, especially if you're drunk.)

6. Talk to your mum and dad. Merely talking about these things means that you could be taking them seriously.

7. If ever your parents offer you a drink, accept it (if you want one, that is). Don't pretend you don't like it just to make them feel better – and don't, for that matter, pretend to like it just to make yourself feel grown up.

8. One of your greatest fears should be getting into a car being driven by a drunk. Assure your parents (and mean it) that you will ring them if this situation crops up. (This sometimes has the added benefit of allowing you to stay a bit longer at the party.) If you do get into a car with a driver who turns out to be – how shall we say – rat-arsed, you're on your own, there's nothing more anyone can do for you, except pray. One extra tip: if you realise in what state your 'chauffeur' is in time, and there's nothing you can do to stop them driving, pretend you feel like throwing up, just as you're about to pull away. Nobody wants sick all over their car (especially if it's their dad's), not even a drunk.

9. The same applies to getting into a car with your parents when they've been drinking. Always tell your parents if you think they're going to drink too much to

drive safely. If they've got any sense they'll thank you and it will show them they can trust you to be sensible. If they haven't, they could well kill someone.

10. Talk to them. Keep the lines of communication open. Leave things around (pamphlets, magazines that you've read, etc.) that show that you might know what you're talking about. If they ask why you've got them, tell them you're fed up with all the lack of information, and often misinformation, about drugs, etc. Let them know it's because you want to learn what's what for yourself, or you could say you're worried about someone at school who you think might have a problem.

11. Ask, if you dare, about their drug experiences, if they have any. If they think you're all in it together, they could even help you in forming your own views on the subject.

12. If what they know seems OK, and not a load of half-baked nonsense, then please listen to them. Not only will it help you, but it will make them happier too.

CHAPTER NINE

New Bits in New Places

It's a funny thing, but whatever stage you are in your physical, mental or emotional development, you can bet your mum and dad will always be one step behind in recognising it. It's bad enough having to go through it – you shouldn't have to suffer unnoticed. You'd think they'd be more clued up, seeing as they live with you, but most parents only see what they want to see.

One of the problems is that the age that people first become aware or interested in things sexual varies enormously. Whoever invented the human being must have had a bit of a giggle. If we were frogs, our mums and dads would be able to tell us exactly at what stage of our development we'd be at any age (having been a tadpole, then a frog themselves). Humans are different.

Most first-time parents would benefit from a kind of

workshop or manual telling them exactly when their little Jimmy would get his first spot, first pubic hair and first erection. It would make it a lot easier to understand what he was going through at any given time. They'd simply be able to look it up on a chart. 'I say, Jimmy will be having his first sexual fantasies this month,' or, 'Ah! It's three months since Annie's birthday – her breasts should start growing this week.'

The trouble is, we know life isn't like that. We develop at different speeds and to different levels of maturity. It wouldn't be that much of a problem if we weren't so ageist, but to teenagers physical maturity is everything. If you're a boy with a long one, you laugh at the mate with a short one and the first body hair is shown off as if the owner's been given it as a prize. As for girls, nothing short of a twenty-one gun salute could do justice to the arrival of boobs.

Very often, however, our physical development straggles along behind where our heads are. We might be receiving a brainful of very rude thoughts, for instance, but our bodies often don't fully understand what to do with them. So you might not feel able to put your feelings into words and discuss them with your parents. Therefore, often the only way your parents manage to catch on, if you're a boy, to your oncoming maturity is from the under-the-bed 'literature', the snigger at a rude joke on the TV, or the long periods of time locked in your room. For girls, it could be when parents notice the hungry looks you get from boys in the street.

I often wonder if humans are the only species who find sex enjoyable? If you are ever at the zoo, or happen to watch one of those tedious wildlife programmes, you see that animals appear to do it as a matter of course, to make babies. They certainly don't seem to get much of a buzz from it. But maybe *that* is what's got your parents' knickers in a twist. Maybe, because sex is so closely connected to reproduction (*especially* if you don't take precautions), it is just too serious for them to joke about.

Talking It Over

Parents feel inhibited and embarrassed about talking about sex with their children, especially with their sons. The irony in this is plain for all to see. Parents have generally been reasonably happy to let their 'sexually naïve' teenagers devour movies where killing, maiming and the dismembering of body parts are par for the course, but will shuffle uncomfortably or go and make the tea if two lusty llamas start bonking on a serious wildlife programme. A good way of proving this is to

watch their expression if you are ever seen to understand a dirty joke or a reference to something rude on the telly. Whether they find it funny or not themselves is most definitely not the point – they find it difficult to believe that you, their innocent child, could possibly know what you're laughing at.

Conversations like this go on all the time:

Mother: I found something rather horrid when I was looking for cups under your bed.

Son: Oh no, don't say you've found my secret stash of drugs.

Mother: Look, I'm not joking. It was a rather unpleasant magazine, with lots of naked women . . .

Son: Oh, that's all right. It isn't mine. *(Nice one. Appear casual at all times.)*

Mother: I don't care whose it is. It's disgusting. Why have you got it, anyway? Do you find those girls attractive? They're so awfully common. Surely they aren't the sort you want to go out with?

Son (embarrassed): Look, I don't know. Why can't you leave me alone?

Mother: Anyway, you shouldn't be interested in that sort of thing at your age. I wonder what your father would say if he knew you had it?

Son (to himself): He'd probably be relieved, seeing as I took it from the stash in his shed.

Parent's View

I really don't understand. How can he find those tarts such a turn-on? I thought he only liked nice girls. I mean, what sort of girl would display her private parts in public like that? Where did we go wrong? I'm sure his father never had stuff like that, otherwise he'd never have chosen someone like me. I bet it's the influence of the company he keeps. I know he wouldn't be filling his head with it if it weren't for his friends at school.

Teenager's View

Oh hell! Nought out of ten for hiding things. I suppose if I kept my room tidy she wouldn't keep going in and looking. As for me, I reckon I'd better stick to the Internet from now on – at least it's easier to hide.

Just remember . . .

At some point during our lives, most of our parents have done the old ostrich thing where talking about sex is concerned – stuck their head in the sand. When that happens most teenagers struggle on, looking elsewhere for the essential information that they need. Remaining ignorant, just because you're not encouraged to make enquiries about sex at home, can lead to all sorts of trouble – unwanted pregnancies and sexually-transmitted infections, for example. See page 98 for places you can go for information or help.

You're Not the Only One

Just as you are having to cope with the changes in your mind and body, your parents, bless 'em, are also having to cope with changes in theirs. And that, my friends, is exactly what your poor old mum and dad are doing now, if they did but know it.

After hours of complex calculations I've worked out that if you are between thirteen and, let's say, seventeen, and your mum and dad had you when they were, let's say, between twenty and forty, then they must be between their late thirties and fifties now (all prizes for mathematics gratefully received). As you yourself are rushing to achieve an age when you'll be taken remotely seriously, your poor old mum and dad are hanging on for dear life to the last vestiges of their youth. By now your poor old grandparents are beginning to show advanced signs of wear and tear. This might not be much of a hassle for you, but for your parents (their children) it's a savage reminder of where they're going.

All the little physical complaints that will probably bug your parents for the rest of their lives begin to present themselves. Energy levels start to flag, often compensated for by vicious bouts of pointless exercise. When they look in the mirror, all they'll ever see are more lines. They're never going to look any better, never going to be more agile or have more energy and never going to be any more attractive to the opposite sex. If they have not reached the point in their careers that they once hoped for, they're probably not going to reach it now. How tragic is all that?

Please don't laugh. There's nothing sadder than a

middle-aged jogger half creeping, half stumbling along the street in a brand-new tracksuit that will, no doubt, be relegated to gardening-wear before the month's out. They'd all do far better to look at the real killer: stress, which lurks behind every unpaid bill. Anyone who tells you that growing older is only a wonderful and life-enriching experience is talking through a part of their anatomy not designed for that purpose.

Your Changing Dad

When a man starts to get to his mid-to-late thirties, weird things begin to happen to his face and body. Those little lines caused by laughing and frowning turn into deep wrinkles; his chin shows signs of growing a double; his waist mysteriously disappears; and if he drinks beer, he begins to get the sort of stomach which, if he was a woman, might lead you to expect a little brother or sister in the not too distant future.

Features such as noses and ears start to grow larger and sprout inappropriate hair. His proper head-hair starts to recede and wear thin and if he has a big problem with it, he'll start to dye it some unnatural colour or, worse still, comb the strands over the bald bit on top. If he shows signs of wanting a hairpiece or wig, you must gently warn him that there has never been one that can't be spotted at fifty yards with one eye closed. If you do, however, make sure there are no sharp objects around.

As for his eyes, they will start to give out and he will probably avoid wearing glasses for as long as possible. He will become confused as to what sort of clothes he should wear and the results can often be hilarious as he tries to mix stuff meant for youngsters with the sort of thing you get in boring old department stores.

Your Changing Mum

If it's bad for men, it's even worse for women. We live in a society that continually tries to convince us that young is beautiful and many women, at quite an early age, embark on a whole load of often expensive measures supposed to keep them looking much younger than they really are. Most are doomed from the outset, as ageing, like many other things, is inevitable. Where do we start?

Firstly there's the dreaded cellulite: that horrid crinkly, wobbly, almost indestructible fat that creeps around supermarkets and coffee mornings looking for women to attach itself to. And how funny is this? As some women are spending fortunes having it sucked out, others are spending even more having plastic substitutes pumped into other areas that nature has rendered lacking.

But that's just the beginning, as well as all the things their male counterparts have to put up with, they have to deal with droopy breasts, coarsening skin, thickening or thinning necks, you name it . . . and far worse: all the bogus cosmetic companies that rob them blind by convincing them that the ageing process is reversible when it isn't.

The Long and Gloomy Road

However you cut it, this will be your mum and dad in the next few years – and just to complicate things further, they will try most of all to hide it from each other. The great difference between the physical changes you are going through and theirs is that while you are on the way up, so to speak, they are on the long and gloomy road down. But hold on a minute. That's if you believe all that propaganda that insists that only young is beautiful. This is a very sad reflection on our society, but you try telling that to the advertisers, magazine and tabloid newspaper publishers or the producers of those ghastly makeover programmes on telly.

If all this isn't enough to deal with, most men and women, after about thirty-five, seem to need a great deal of reassurance that they are still as attractive as they were (even if they aren't!).

On the Bright Side

As for yourself, cheer up. You won't always have a complexion like the surface of the moon, you probably won't get so hairy that the only career opportunity will be with a passing circus, or stay so hairless (if you're a boy) that you'll never need to shave. If you are a girl, rest assured you will almost certainly have something worth putting in a bra, and not always resemble a garden rake.

Doing It for the First Time

You'd better take this on board right away. Even if you think your parents are the most liberal and progressive in the world, when the subject of sex rears its ugly head, they'll almost certainly turn out like everyone else's. If your mum and dad ever found it hard talking about how and where babies came from, it'll be nothing compared to broaching the subject of actually 'doing it'.

Some parents are so embarrassed that they contrive to make sure the subject is never mentioned. In fact, the way they go on, it probably wouldn't surprise you to learn that your mother had been visited by an angel and that you were the 'second coming' – the result of a virgin birth. The subject is so taboo in some households that it is not unknown for young people to approach their mid-to-late teens still a little shaky on the details of what exactly goes on in the sex and reproduction department.

Sex and Parents (Yuck!)

The idea of your mum and dad actually doing it has to be a bit weird if not a bit disgusting. I mean, why *would* they?

Keeping a healthy and fun sex life going for a long time ain't easy. It's a bit like playing a new computer game. At first it's exciting and brill, but once you've played it a couple of hundred times the fascination can go. The point I'm trying to make is that while you're reaching your peak as far as sexual libido is concerned, your parents are on the way down. For this reason alone, they might find it difficult to talk about, because they might simply not remember what it was like to have sex be a driving force in their lives.

Sex and You (Gulp!)

Your parents' hang-up is quite simple. The average mummy and daddy find it almost impossible to put over to their little ones, that sticking what their nippers regard as one rude bit into someone else's rude bit, and then jiggling it around, could possibly be regarded as interesting (let alone fun!). I don't know about you, but when I first heard of the sexual act when I was little, I saw it as some ghastly chore that one day I would have to endure if I ever wanted children of my own. The idea that I might want to go through it as many times as possible, *avoiding* making babies, would have seemed completely baffling.

Whether you look at all those books with drawings that resemble soft pink engine parts when you're young, or the cold, rather clinical, approach you get at school, you'll get the idea that you'll probably need a set of instructions when the time comes (like building a wardrobe from a kit). The alternative – hearing about it in wildly inaccurate detail from your schoolmates, is worse. Isn't it crazy? All this to describe what man and woman have been doing since Adam first got it right with Eve (snakes and all).

Jeez, it's enough to put us *all* off!

So Why the Big Prob?

It all stems from the fact that your parents have had you from new, so to speak. To them you are still, underneath it all, the innocent little baby they brought into the world to love and to cherish. It's only a relatively short time since they were leaning over your cot making daft goo-goo noises and even less since they were reading you stories about bunny-rabbits and baa-lambs. Now they're faced with passing on the explicit details of what they actually did to make you. It's one thing telling your kids the process that must be gone through to make children, but it all becomes different when they realise that you might be anxious to get on with it:

Mother *(gingerly holding a packet of condoms):* I found these in the drawer next to your bed. What in heaven's name are you doing with them?

Girl: What are you doing going through my stuff? It's nothing to do with you.

Mother: So who is it to do with, may I ask? Anyway, you're far too young. Why should you want to do something like that? Has that Ben put you up to it? You haven't been going too far, have you?

Girl: Course not – it's just in case.

Mother: In case of what? You shouldn't even be thinking of things like that. I'd better ring his mother. *(Thinks to herself: before wringing Ben's neck!)*

Girl: Oh no, Mum, please don't. You'll make me look a right idiot. Look, why don't you stop treating me like a kid. Sooner or later we're going to want to. Isn't it better to take precautions now – before it's too late?

Mother: I said it before, you're just too young to even be thinking about such things. I know your father agrees with me.

Parent's View

Damn, damn, damn – that caught me right on the hop. I never thought she was anywhere near that stage. I was pretty sure they were into heavy snogging, but I thought it stopped there. What should we do for the best? The trouble with kids these days is that if you try to stop them, they'll just go and do it anyway and then we'll either be premature grandparents or there'll be an abortion to deal with. I was eighteen before I even thought of going all the way, and that was with her father. What will *he* think? God, he'll go ballistic when I tell him – she's still a baby in his eyes. I doubt whether he even realises she's mature physically, let alone poised on the brink. Let's hope this Ben thing's a five minute wonder like all the others. With a bit of luck there'll be someone else in a few weeks.

Teenager's View

Talk about sticking your head in the sand. I wouldn't mind betting she thinks we play on PlayStations or Doctors and Nurses when I go round to Ben's. She should be relieved that I'm even thinking about preventing pregnancy and STIs. She'd go through the roof if she had any idea how close we'd got, and that it was once a very near thing (about three seconds away!). Don't they know that things have changed and people don't wait for a wedding ring any more. Blimey, I'm seventeen – if I leave it any longer they'll be making room for me in a nunnery. Anyway, why don't they realise that I really love Ben and there'll never be anyone else?

So What Next?

Most parents are completely at sea when it comes to situations like this, and would rather jump ship than face it. It is a no-win situation. If they agree to you taking precautions, they might feel as if it's as good as giving you a free permit to sleep with anyone you like, when you like. On the other hand, if they go too heavily the other way they'll worry that you'll do it without protection and that any ensuing pregnancy could be their fault. What's sad is that they've forgotten the intensity of passion (and plain lust) that you feel at your age. You you might not be ready to have sex even if you're having sexy thoughts, but it's just as well to be prepared for when the day comes.

Much as you might feel curious, or impatient, to find out what real sex is like, it'll be your parents' intention to keep you from it for as long as possible. The real trouble is that there's no such time as 'ready' where sex is concerned. All one can suggest you do when you finally get round to it is that you do it with:

1. Someone you really care for (who feels the same way about you) and feel you can talk to (which rules out bonking someone you've met five minutes ago).
2. Someone you trust (who isn't going to shout the details out to the whole neighbourhood and will understand if you change your mind at the last minute).
3. Someone who you are pretty sure you'll want to see again after you've done it (and will want to see you).
4. Someone with at least as much self-control as you have (so you'll *both* be thinking about having safe sex).

Timing

If you remember anything from this chapter, remember this: There's plenty of time for the real thing. It isn't a race, and there isn't a medal at the end of it. There are a thousand and one things you can do without going all the way and some of them feel just as good. Don't let your friends try to make you feel a sissy if you haven't yet (chances are they're exaggerating about their experiences anyway), and if you are going to do it . . . USE A CONDOM to protect against STIs and unwanted pregnancy. In this day and age if you don't, you need your head (and your blood) examined.

Finally, if you think you could be the last teenager on earth not to have had sex, take heart. Research shows that at least some of your mates are not being completely honest about their sexual experiences anyway. Surely it's better to wait than to regret anything?

How to Deal With the Poor Old Things

1. Find better places to hide your dirty magazines!
2. Let your parents be aware, even if it is a bit embarrassing, that you *are* interested in sex.
3. Try not to be one of those teenagers (like I was!) who avoid the rude bits on telly when watching with your parents. Don't run out of the room, or suddenly start playing with the dog, or flicking through the *TV Times*. They'll think you're embarrassed – or worse: just not mature enough to be interested. If one of them gets trigger happy with the remote, tell them

not to change it on your account. Another way of letting them know that you know what they know, is to laugh with them if something rude comes up in conversation or on the telly – especially if it's by way of a double meaning. It might be a bit awkward at first, but let's face facts: it could be the first time they realise that you understand about sex.

4. Introduce them to girlfriends and boyfriends as soon as you feel confident with your relationship. Boys especially often pretend, for some reason I can't understand (even though I was the same), that they're just not interested in girls. It's a sort of junior macho thing. If your parents are the kind that give you a hard time over the opposite sex, you can bet your last ten pence that it's because they're having an even harder time with your growing up than you are.

5. If you are having real problems with anything involving your body, changes or puberty, and feel you can't talk to the old folk, go see your school nurse, doctor or consider ringing a helpline or visting a family planning clinic. Don't be embarrassed – these people deal with this sort of stuff every day. It's like taking your car to a garage for them (except garages charge you a fortune and most times get it wrong). Also look at websites for more information.

6. These are probably the major fears your parents have relating to you and sex:

   a) You've been there already!

   b) That you did it, or look like you're about to do it with someone they really can't stand.

   c) That if you do it, you'll end up pregnant or getting someone pregnant or catching an STI.

   As such, it's a good idea to reassure them that you are thinking about the subject seriously.

7. When talking to the old folk, bring them to the subject gently so as not to shock them or put them off their supper. Maybe mention something you read about in a magazine or saw on telly. Try asking their opinion.

8. If they go off on one, don't panic. Let them know that you only mentioned it so as to be as informed as possible. Try to listen to what they have to say. It will make them realise that you are prepared to hear more than one side of the argument. They may seem overprotective to you, but they are aware of the risks involved and might actually be a good source of information.

9. If you feel you just can't talk to your parents about such things, then go to reputable and reliable sources for information. The following websites and phone numbers might be some help to you:

fpa (Family Planning Association)

(Can send you free leaflets and guides on contraception, STIs, periods, puberty and lots more besides, or confidential information and advice.)

Tel: 0845 3101334

www.fpa.org.uk

Sexwise

(Confidential advice to under 18s on sex, relationships and contraception.)

Tel: 0800 567 123 (Open 24/7)

www.ruthinking.co.uk

10. Remember, if you think that telling them might cause World War Three, then don't. Only you can know whether you have the sort of parents who'd like to know and can deal with it or not.

(**Girls be warned:** your dad would probably disapprove of Prince Charming if he thought he was going to bonk his precious daughter.)

CHAPTER TEN

Meeting the Parents

Isn't life odd? For years nothing you do ever seems right to your mum and dad, but when you bring your first boyfriend (or girlfriend) home, you're suddenly the little angel being corrupted by the kid from hell. Daughters, it must be said, get a much harder time of it than sons. Here's how the conversations can go:

Dad: So that was the Dominic we've been hearing all about. I must admit, we were a bit taken aback.

Daughter: Why? Didn't you think he was cool?

Dad: That's hardly the word I'd use. All we needed to go on was what he looks like. Let's face it he's never going to win Britain's Best Turned-out Boy, is he?

Daughter: Dom's great when you get to know him, Dad. You're such a hypocrite. You always told me never to judge a book by its cover.

Dad: He was like a rather moth-eaten cover, with no pages inside.

Daughter: You're so horrible. I can't think what sort of boy you'd like. Probably a teenage Tony Blair.

Dad: Well, I suppose if *you* like him, there's not much more to be said, but I really think you could do better.

Daughter (thinks): I expect Dom thinks I could do much better, dad-wise.

THIS IS DOM, DAD!

Parent's View

I know it sounds pathetic, but I can't bear the idea of that spotty little oik getting his hands on my daughter. How could she find him attractive? I've met tortoises with more get-up-and-go. It wouldn't be so bad if he had something to say for himself, but he acted as if his brain had just been removed. I don't expect her to go out with the winner of *Mastermind*, but *some* sort of mind would help.

Teenager's View

Well, that was a huge success. Why couldn't they give him a break? It turned out like an interview. Anyone would think he was applying for a job, the way my dad went on. You could tell Dom was shy, but did Dad take that into consideration? No way. It's so unfair – Dom's a right laugh when he's with our mates, but obviously doesn't do parents. That really is the last time I bring anyone home. I don't give a damn what they think any more.

Parent Power

You disagree with a lot of what your parents say, but still, when it comes right down to it, most kids seek their parents' approval. This, you will be mega-depressed to learn, could well go into adulthood. Maybe the real definition of a proper grown-up is someone who at last doesn't lose sleep about what their parents think. Some poor devils never achieve this and are dominated by their parents for most of their lives, even when they're married with kids of their own.

A Few Tips

If you are considering presenting the current love of your life to your parents or, even more daunting, are going to see his or hers, there are a few things you can do to make it more bearable:

1. If you're the one in the strange house, try not to be scared of the parents. In some way they could be more scared of you. It's you they're worried will lead their little darling astray (with a bit of luck), not them.
2. Try, try, try to talk. Anything's better than silence. The less you say, the more they think you've something to hide. There's nothing worse than someone who simply mumbles one-word answers. However, be warned that chattering away about meaningless things won't show you or your boy/girlfriend in

your best light. Try to relax, and remember that they'd probably prefer to like you or your boy/girl-friend than not.

3. Don't whisper and giggle amongst yourselves when in the same room as the parents. If anything's guaranteed to get up their noses, it's that.

4. If you are of the male gender, you can bet your bottom dollar that your girlfriend's dad will be thinking that all you want to do is get your grubby hands on his precious daughter's body. This may well be true, but for goodness' sake, don't begin to do it in front of them. Try and keep at least six inches apart on the first meeting. That way, it might not be the last.

5. When visiting your boy/girlfriend's parents, try to tone down your appearance for the first few times. If your nose, eyebrows, ears and tongue are full of metal, take the jewellery out for the day. First impressions are everything in this game.

6. If it's your boy/girlfriend in the hotseat, make up a compliment he/she could possibly have (though probably didn't) made to you about how nice your parents seemed. Make sure you get this in first before your parents launch into any attack. It should stop them in their tracks – at least for a bit!

Nobody's Perfect

If you remember this and nothing else, try to get it into your head that nobody can ever be good enough from a parent's point of view. If you make no effort at all, the meeting is bound to go badly and if you try too hard you could end up making things just as bad. All you can be is yourself so don't oversell it or undersell it.

Best of luck – you might need it.

CHAPTER ELEVEN

Beware — Aliens!

Some of the greatest problems facing young people of your age occurs when it becomes obvious that your mother and father really aren't getting on. I'd like to be able to say that there are ways that you can help the situation, but I am at a loss. All I can suggest is that you try not to take sides and avoid at all costs getting involved in their arguments. Hopefully, it will be just a bad patch and they will weather the storm, but if the worst does happen, it can be really difficult for all involved.

Love or Marriage?

Getting married is like buying a second-hand car: all bright and shiny when you first get in it, but after a while, things can start going wrong, That old 'till death do us part' guarantee that you give each other when you get married sometimes isn't worth the paper it's printed on (a bit like the one you get with a car).

If your parents decide to separate, you're not alone. Statistics show that these days, less than half of marriages survive.

The End of the Era

Here's the scenario. One minute you're living in perfect discord with your mum and dad, bickering, sulking and all the other stuff that goes on in normal family life, and the next minute one or other of them decides to quit the happy home. Worse – they might move in with someone else. Having a new adult in your life to replace the one that has gone creates a whole new set of problems.

Mother: Tom, darling, I'm afraid I have got some rather important news.

Son: Don't say you're going to start getting on.

Mother: Your father has decided to live somewhere else.

Son: Who with?

Mother: I'm afraid it's someone he met at the office. I didn't want to have to tell you, darling.

Son: Is that why he's been coming home so late?

Mother: It looks that way. I'm so sorry. We'll survive, but I guess you're going to be the man of the house.

Parent's View

Poor kid. It must be really tough for him. Whatever happens between me and his father is down to us – he's had nothing to do with it. I wish I had some control over the situation, but the ball's not in my court. Anyway, I'm not sure I could have him back after this.

Teenager's View

I had a feeling things were going pear-shaped, but I didn't think it was as bad as this. I could kill Dad for ruining our lives! Why couldn't he just get it out of his system and then carry on as normal. I think Mum's being very brave, but I bet she's hurting underneath. I'm never getting bloody married.

BEWARE — ALIENS!

Whose Fault Is It Anyway?

Marriages can go stale for all sorts of reasons. It's important to remember that parental break-ups and bad marriages are certainly not your fault, no matter how you think you might have behaved — they are due to problems between adults.

Welcome?

You might have thought your parents were naff, boring and bossy and all that, but at least they were *your* parents, which gave them some sort of privilege to behave like that. It takes a long time to accept someone else telling you what to do, especially on your own patch.

The conversation about the father who has been — how shall we put it? — 'working late' is quite common. But it's not always the case that one party is solely to blame for the break-up. And it probably won't seem long before the 'innocent party' starts dating, and if you're *really* unlucky, before you've had time to get used to that idea, there's someone new popping round to your house to take over where your other parent left off.

How bad is that? If we were animals, we wouldn't hear of it (we'd either scare 'em off or eat 'em). Unfortunately, we don't get the choice and are supposed

109

to keep quiet and accept the situation. Kids are usually expected to fit in with their parents' lives whether they want to or not – never the other way round. Mind you, to be fair, it's not only a pain in the butt for you. It's almost worse for the parent who's bringing in the trespasser or – dare I say – the trespasser him or herself! But surely, I hear you say, that's *their* problem.

Mother: Mark, darling, you could at least try to make Neville welcome. It's not easy for him . . . or me, come to that.

Teenager: C'mon, Mum. It's his and your choice, not mine. I can't remember having a say in it.

Mother: Look, I asked you if you'd mind if he moved in, and you just shrugged. I took that to mean a yes.

Teenager: That was before I realised what he was like.

Mother: What do you mean, 'realised what he's like'? I've been seeing Neville for over a year.

Teenager: Yeah, but at least he went home most times. I just can't work out how you could fancy someone like that.

Mother: You're so cruel. Just because he's quiet and sensitive and doesn't throw his weight around . . . unlike *someone else* who used to live here.

Teenager: Just let him try, that's all. This is our house. Isn't it *his* job to fit in with *us*? Look, Mum, he's not my dad and never will be.

Mother: You're so hard on him. I really don't know where it comes from. Neville thinks the world of you. Why can't you at least give him a chance?

Teenager: Look, I'll have a go, but don't you try to make me stick around while he's playing his awful CDs, or asking me to carry his golf clubs round the golf course.

Parent's View

Cunning little devil. I know it can't have been easy when his father ran off like that, but it's been a long time now and he's really milking it. I felt sorry at first, but I don't any more. He knows full well he's got me where he wants me. He's holding Nev's and my happiness in the palm of his hand. I reckon he'll use this one for all it's worth and for as long as he can.

Why does he treat poor Nev as if he's from another planet? Sometimes he completely ignores him when he's talking to him. It's just not fair. His own father would have knocked him into the middle of next week if he'd behaved like that; whereas Nev, poor love, bends over backwards to be understanding . . . and that's why I like him so much. He can only take so much, though, and I'm sure that he'll snap pretty soon. Maybe the sooner the better.

Teenager's View

Jeeeeeesus, what a creep! Nev's a complete, no-holds-barred nerd. How could Mum fancy him? How could a mother of mine go out with someone called 'Neville', for a start? Urggggh! And as for all his terrible jokes – if I found them in some cheap Christmas crackers I'd ask for my money back . . . I can't bear it when he goes into all that understanding 'what-it's-like-to-be-a-teenager, I-used-to-be-one-myself' stuff. Blimey, I can't believe he ever was one. It would be better if he was just his awful self and didn't try to be my mate and stuff – at least we'd know where the battle lines were drawn.

I keep trying to remember how bad it was in this house when Mum and Dad were fighting all the time and then that cold-war period when they didn't talk at all, but I reckon if anything this is worse. Watching the two of them canoodling like a couple of kids, calling each other 'darling' and 'sweetie' and stuff like that, makes me want to throw up. If I was wrecked on a desert island with Neville, I'd end up eating him.

No Solution?

Even if you do grow to like your mum or dad's new partner, he (or she) can seldom replace whoever's gone, however imperfect they might have been. After all, it wasn't *you* who divorced them and it wasn't *you* who had all the arguments. It's not surprising if you prefer the one that had to clear off.

On the other hand, you might be dealing with the ravages of war, so having someone in the house that treats your mother or father well, might be a blessed relief even if it's weird for you.

New Brothers and Sisters

If it's bad enough having to accept a new adult in your life, what if they have kids of their own? You can bet that your mother or father, together with their new partner, will hope you will all get on (because it's so much easier that way). But why should you? One of the rights we have as human beings is to be able to choose our friends, and that's exactly what we do. Just by putting people together doesn't mean they're going to hit it off. If anyone does that to you, unless you are the friendliest person in the world, it's likely to get right up your nose and – remember this – THEIRS TOO! They are in exactly the same leaky boat as you are, if you think about it. Worse still, you never know, they could be thinking exactly the same about your mum or dad as you think of theirs. Maybe knowing that will have the dreaded effect of bringing you closer – it's possible. All you can hope is that you can get something fun out of it ... sometimes laughter can really make awful things seem much better.

How to Handle the Situation Without Murdering Someone

1. Remember that no matter how bad things seem for you, it really isn't your show. Nobody in their right mind *plans* to split up and you can bet that both your mum and dad are going through at least as much hell as you are. They certainly haven't set out to make your life a misery.

2. You must try to establish whether this new person in your life really is a creep, or just someone in an almost impossible situation. There are probably far worse people your parents could have chosen.

3. For the first month or so, everyone will be walking on eggshells, trying not to piss each other off. As the time goes on things will probably settle down, so

don't rock the boat until everybody's been given a chance to settle in.

4. Remember to try and be sensitive to your parents' feelings at this time. Their emotions will be pretty raw and they could well be suffering from a lack of confidence too. So, be a support for them, and you might feel better for it as well.

5. If the new person in the house appears to be over-lenient, letting you get away with murder and stuff, be careful. They're probably trying to get in your good books. It might be OK at first, but a certain amount of strictness can be a good thing. It means a degree of strength and leadership which a) means they care and b) could be ever so useful if you ever get into some real trouble later on.

6. For obvious reasons, you often become the only form of contact between the two of them, albeit indirect, and that can be difficult. One parent might want to know what the other person in their ex-partner's life is like, for instance. If they do, be careful not to slag them off just to make the one who's asking feel better – it can only backfire. Try to give as little information away as possible and if you do speak about it, be careful, especially if you feel you owe loyalty to both of them. You could even ask your parents what they

want you to say if the other parent asks. That would indicate that you are trying to understand how they feel.

Best of Luck

Having your mum and dad split is a horrible thing. Most times, at least one of them is very upset and hurt by the situation and wishes it hadn't happened. Last of all, don't feel like it's up to you to get them back together again. Some people can work through their problems, and others may not be able to, but you can't force something like this.

CHAPTER THIRTEEN

Then and Now

You've probably worked out by now that not getting on with your parents is nothing new, and it's not just something that only happens in your household either. All over the world doors are slamming, horrible things are being said and gallons of tears are being shed . . . and all because parents and teenagers, ever since time began, have had problems communicating. It usually all boils down to respect. Parents seem to think they should have it by right, while teenagers are continually being told they have to earn it.

Does this argument sum it up?

Father: Why is it a struggle whenever I ask you to do something?

Son: Like what?

Father: Oh, I don't know – like coming home on time, or helping us more around the house or doing your homework without being screamed at – you know what I mean. Why don't you ever believe that what I tell you is for your own good? It's as if my experience of life counts for nothing in your world.

Son: C'mon, Dad, look at the mess your generation have got the planet into. Global warming, acid rain, half the world with nothing to eat and the rest as fat as pigs from eating the other's share. And a country where our politicians get us into stupid wars we don't even want by telling porkies. Yeah, Dad – brilliant!

Father: Don't be so cheeky. Anyway, what's all that got to do with it? At least we were taught to respect our parents. If I'd spoken to my father like you speak to me, I'd have been walloped.

Son: Yeah, that's the way I would expect most grown-ups would prefer to settle arguments.

Father: I tell you, you've got a rude awakening coming. You just wait till you've got a family of your own to bring up, or a house to run – then you'll see. A bit of cooperation wouldn't go amiss. When I think what your mum and I sacrificed for you and your brother.

Son (under breath): Oh no. Not the old 'you're so lucky' chestnut again. Please, oh Lord, if you ever hear me saying that crap, zap me!

Parent's View

I wonder if I was the same with my father. I'm sure I must have taken his advice a bit more than that ungrateful little tyke. I can see him about to make the same mistakes as I did, but it's like watching someone driving purposefully over a cliff. If only he would realise that I could help him so much if he'd just listen. The trouble is, this generation have it too easy. Everything they want seems to come on a plate, and are they grateful? You bet they're not.

Teenager's View

I really don't know if I can hack much more of this. He still treats me like a six-year-old. No wonder I can never tell him anything. Where do they get the idea that the older you get, the wiser you become? Adults don't seem to get any clearer about things. I wonder if Einstein had this problem with his dad? Anyway, if that were true, very old people would all be geniuses. You've only got to hear them wittering on to realise how untrue that is.

Dad seems to know nothing about what's going down these days, apart from the golf club and who's doing what with whom at work. It's all right for him, he's through the difficult bit. Why can't he just sit back and enjoy his twilight years ... AND LEAVE ME A-BLOODY-LONE!!!

The Everlasting Generation Gap

It isn't just the way you behave that bugs them, it's the music you listen to, the food you prefer, the clothes you wear and most of all the perceived lack of ambition that they swear they didn't have when they were your age.

Most parents seem to be stuck in a time warp. They believe they lived in a sort of golden age and that everything you can think of is not as good as when they were young. This may in fact be true, but it's hardly your fault. Have a look at the glossary on page 129 and you'll begin to get an idea.

CHAPTER FOURTEEN

Be Lucky!

When I was your age, my parents were so straight that just about everything they did or believed in was something I felt I needed to rebel against. I was expected to work hard at school in order to get a safe job (which I would stay in forever), get married, have two children and vote for whichever political party promised to keep my comfy middle-class life safe and secure.

During the sixties, a large number of newly minted teenagers (like me) looked more closely at their parents' lives and decided: Thank you, but no thank you. They wanted their own lives and so, when they eventually grew up, a new generation of parents was born, who, for the first time, rather liked the idea that their children might turn into their friends rather than people they could simply boss around. Unlike their parents, they'd grown up with televisions, cars and without the constant threat of having to go to war to fight someone for some cause that really wasn't anything to do with them. For once, owing to the possibility of extending their education, they didn't have to go to work at sixteen to do exactly what their parents suggested for a living. Best of all, they decided that they didn't have to share their parents' beliefs if they disagreed with them.

The trouble is that parents like myself (for this was my generation) were still the products of this fairly strict do-as-I-say upbringing, and although we tried our level best to adopt this new approach, we found it hard sometimes to adjust to *our* teenagers who knew nothing of that past world where parents were always right. Added to this, of course, is the undeniable truth that within most teenagers are various degrees of rebellion.

What About Politics?

Unlike many of their parents, who literally voted the way their parents had voted, kids today seldom believe what our beloved politicians tell them. To be honest, they no longer even listen. Ask amongst your friends who the leaders of the main parties are, and what they believe in, and they probably wouldn't have a clue. By the time you lot reach the voting age, you probably won't be bothered – and who can blame you? But this plays exactly into the politicians' hands. The apathy caused by successive governments, who seem to pay practically no attention to what the people who voted them in actually asked for, is evident in the poor turnout at election time. The only way this can change, however, is if young people like you begin to look more closely at those in power and start demanding to know how and why they got there, and what they plan to do.

And Religion?

Fewer teenagers than ever follow a religion and so, rather than argue about it (which can lead to massive conflict in very religious families), tend to ignore the subject completely. According to a National Opinion Poll in 1999, seventy-seven per cent of eight-year-olds have no faith at all and I very much doubt whether things have changed much since then.

Many people believe the fewer than eight per cent of British people who do still go to church belong to a world that doesn't seem to exist any more, and on top of that, it doesn't take a genius to recognise that throughout the world, religion is probably as responsible for as many of the horrid things that go on as anything else. The increasingly violent feuding between the Muslim world and the Jewish or Christian worlds, for example, becomes more and more incomprehensible to those who don't believe in any of it in the first place.

If wars about who you believe in are ridiculous, then so are those about political ideologies. As far as I and hopefully you are concerned, wars are simply things that other people do, and quite right too. If there was ever again a compulsory call to arms of Britain's youth, it would be very interesting to see what the reaction would be.

And the Media?

Every decade or so, the media hang labels on the young people of the day – there were the Teddy boys and beat-niks of the fifties, to the mods and rockers of the sixties, the hippies of the early seventies and the punks of the late seventies and early eighties. If there is no argument on a clear label for the youth of the nineties and beyond – in other words, you lot! – I would like to think that this is because what you are into is far too complex and sophisticated for the prattling and prattish newspaper writers to get their heads round. That's why they only seem to concentrate on the yobs and pond-life and, by so doing, make out that they represent British youth.

We owe rock and roll for teaching us that a youth culture was at least possible, but unfortunately it provided very little else apart from a depressing fascination with celebrity. Hippies taught us that being good, and peaceful protest were ways of rebelling against our stupid warmongering elders, but got so caught up in mind-bending drugs and silly clothes that, in the end, no one took them seriously. The punks taught us that anyone from any level of society could do anything they wanted, but became so obsessed with trying to shock the papers that they eventually traded in their anger for self-publicity and column inches. Unlike past movements, your generation, who don't get so obsessed in fly-by-night trends that supposedly define you, could be the first that have a real future.

So What's the Point?

Most kids today don't seem to want to shock anyone, change anyone or be forced into anything they don't want to do. And if you are anything like them, you don't particularly want to campaign against all the wrongs in the world, but at the same time, you don't want to cause any. All you want is to be as happy as possible and enjoy life – and what's wrong with that?

I hope, after reading this book, that one of the elements that often stands in the way of this worthwhile pursuit – your parents – might be slightly easier to handle. If they aren't, then please remember, when you are in the same position as them (perish the thought) go a littler easier on *your* teenagers. You know it makes sense!

Some Final Advice on How to Handle the Parents

1. Parents worry, it's a fact. It's sort of what they're for! That's why they are always needing to ask questions that are sometimes impossible to answer. There are two ways to tackle these. The 'good way' will get the persistent parent problem off your back, while the 'bad way' will simply make them even more anxious, resulting in even more questions. So, if you prefer peace, not war, consider your answers carefully.
2. Look for all those tell-tale signs of stress. If you know they're having a hard time financially, try to adjust your demands accordingly (ask for an fifty quid pair of trainers rather than ninety!). Seriously, they may not show it, but most parents hate not being able to buy their kids those little luxuries that,

at the time, you don't think you can possibly live without. Either that or they're just plain mean!

3. If you can help boost your own pocket money, without dealing drugs or robbing banks, it will show them that you don't think money grows on trees (it grows in deposit accounts).

4. Most parents, despite how it might appear, don't want to spoil things for you. A little reassurance can go a long way.

5. Try not to look miserable all the time. You'd be surprised the effect a smiling face can have round the house.

6. In order to keep the old dears happy, pay them compliments now and again and try to take their feelings into consideration (they may not actually enjoy all the washing, ironing, housework, cooking and errand-running, not to mention having to earn all the money).

7. See if you can find some things that you like doing together, even if it's only mooching around the shops or taking the dog to the park. Sharing time away from all the stresses of domestic life might help them see you as a person and not just a pain in the neck.

8. Get it into your head that your parents do daft things just like you – even if they won't admit it. They might sometimes drink too much, waste money on

things they don't really need, say the wrong things at family gatherings, pay too much attention to a members of the opposite sex – you name it. After all, they're not another species, just human beings like you – only thirty or so years on and just trying, again like you are, to make head or tail of it all.

GLOSSARY

If your parents are in their forties or fifties now, there are some major and just downright weird things that they have lived through and that have influenced their tastes, values and the times they lived in. If they seem bizarre, then maybe you'll understand their feelings about the things that interest you. The following are some of the events and fashions that helped shape the back end of the last century. Some you will heard of, some you won't.

1950s

What a Dreadful Carry On?

You either loved 'em or you hated 'em. The *Carry On* films were thought to be hilarious by many in your parents' generation. Some of us, however, thought they were about as funny as a wet Sunday in Slough. The first, *Carry On Sergeant,* was made in 1958 and many people (like me) believe it should have been burned at birth. Unbelievably they made a total of thirty-one films, finishing with *Carry on Columbus* in 1992 which was, incredibly, even less funny than the rest.

Britain the Great

Nobody who saw it could forget the wonderful Festival of Britain in 1951. Held on the south bank of the Thames in the Battersea Pleasure Gardens, it celebrated all that was great about post-war British design in the arts, science and technology (and there was also a fab funfair).

Upwards and Upwards

Everyone seemed to go mountain crazy in 1953 when Edmund Hillary and a guide called Tenzing Norgay managed to get to the top of Everest, the world's highest mountain – we even got the day off from school. Now so many people go up and down it, I wouldn't be surprised if they opened a McDonald's at the top.

No Smoking

The first ever links between cancer and cigarette smoking were established in 1954. From that point on, if anyone chose to smoke, it was at their own risk.

Deb's Delight

There used to be a strange ceremony, which thankfully came to an end in 1958, involving girls (called 'debutantes') from the smartest and richest families in the country being presented to the Queen. It was basically a cattle-market for wealthy young men (the 'deb's delights') to get a peek at what was on offer – before committing themselves.

1960s

Buy One and Stop One

The beginning of the permissive era could be said to have begun with a bang in January 1961 when the first female contraceptive pill came on the market. Suddenly women could take decisive action for themselves, without having to rely on their partners.

Is this Really It?

Anyone who lived through the Cuba crisis in 1962 will understand what it's like to be on the brink of disaster. World War Three and a total holocaust never seemed so close. Mr Kruschev, the Russian president, had built hundreds of nuclear missiles on the island of Cuba and pointed them straight at America only ninety miles away.

The Fab Beatles

Nothing prepared Britain or the world for the phenomena that were known as The Beatles. One minute they were just a small group in an English northern town but by 1964 they were our biggest export. Parents didn't really approve of the hysteria, but anything was better than the disgraceful Rolling Stones who were beginning to gain a reputation (albeit a bad one) in London.

Mini Fever

Britain went mini-mad in the sixties. First it was designer Mary Quant's miniskirt that brought traffic to a halt. Then, by the end of the decade, half the actual traffic on the road seemed to be Minis. The fabulous Mini car, designed by Alec Issigonis for Morris Motors, was an instant hit.

Moon Men

One minute we were looking at the man in the moon, and the next there were actually real men *on* the moon. Americans Neil Armstrong and Buzz Aldrin made their

first momentous steps in July 1969. We all thought that
we would soon be visiting other planets and talking to
men with two heads.

The Cold War

After the Second World War, a puzzling new confrontation began to take place. It became known as the Cold
War, because no actual fighting took place, only the
waving of nuclear weapons. The two sides were very
clearly defined – the communists, led by Russia and
China, versus the capitalists, led by the United States.

Peace and Love

Perhaps the strongest, most visual youth movement ever
to hit Britain began in the late sixties and carried
through into the seventies. The progeny of politicians
and dustmen alike 'turned on and tuned out' on a wave
of marijuana and LSD. Fashion-wise, it was a riot –
anything seemed to go with anything, in a psychedelic
mishmash of colour and fabric. It was at this time that all
the huge music festivals began, much to the distress of
parents throughout the country, who thought they
would never see their offspring again. Boys grew their
hair long, wore beads, headbands and flared trousers,
while girls put flowers in their hair, wore floaty frocks

and went around barefoot. Both sexes bared their chests, painted their bodies and gyrated as if possessed by demons at any given opportunity. While hippiedom in the US (which produced the Woodstock festival) was billed as a youth protest against the Vietnam War, it was more likely to have been an excuse for upsetting the generation that got them into it.

The Vietnam War

It really kicked off in 1965 when US combat troops arrived and the States, via new president Lyndon B. Johnson, adopted the self-styled role of protector of the free world, by taking on the might of the communist bloc. He tried to stop the Chinese-backed North Vietnamese from swallowing up the rest of the relatively small country. The Americans thought if they got away with it here, it would start a domino effect causing many more little countries to succumb to the dastardly communists. It was a war they could never win, particularly as most of their soldiers, thousands of miles from home, never really had their hearts in it. Hearts in it or not, 15,685 young American lives ended along with two million Vietnamese. Thank God the British never got involved (I bet we would these days). Despite what our politicians wanted, however, it is generally agreed that if such a meaningless and calamitous conflict happened today, this generation would refuse to go and fight. Quite right too.

Elvis – the King of Rock and Roll

Do you get sick of your parents (or their parents, even) going on about Elvis Presley, the King of Rock and Roll? It seems ironic when you consider that he was worshipped almost as a god, for when he started out, the sounds he made were referred to as the Devil's music in the Bible-bashing southern states where he hailed from. Either way, when the most famous rock and roll star died on August 16th 1977, he was far from the sleek hip-wiggler that all the ladies went silly over. He ended up as fat as a pudding, having lived on a diet of burgers, Coke and barbiturates for the last few years of his life.

Andrew Lloyd Webber

Composer Lloyd Webber is one of the great dividers today between kids and their parents. First Sirred and then Lorded, Lloyd Webber was almost single-handedly responsible for a bunch of musicals (for want of a better word) that for some reason people of your parents' generation and older seemed to find worthy of parting with good money to go see. They included *Joseph and the Amazing Technicolor Dreamcoat* (1968), *Evita* (1978), *Cats* (1981) and *The Phantom of the Opera* (1986).

1970s

The Full Monty

Monty Python's Flying Circus, perhaps the most groundbreaking (not to mention wacky) comedy series ever to be seen on British television, hit our screens in late 1969 and dominated the early seventies. Humour was never to be the same again. So many of the award-winning series around today seem to owe so much to *Python*'s crazy approach.

Men Beware

A huge movement started in the early seventies, by women, for women. Known as 'Women's Liberation', it was a reaction against the treatment women had received from men since time began. Bras were even burned as a symbol of protest and freedom. Although not nearly as strident today, no one could deny that Women's Lib was largely responsible for increasing equality in the workplace that women enjoy today.

Four Days Off

In 1973, the Tory government under Edward Heath, decided to take on the miners' leaders who were refusing to let their workers do overtime. It resulted in the ridiculous three-day week which meant that businesses could only use electricity on selected days and the general public were subjected to crippling power cuts at home. Many people, like myself, seriously considered emigration.

Bye, Bye, Benny

The Benny Hill Show, popular throughout the seventies and eighties, was about as vulgar as you could get and only funny if you enjoyed watching the ageing comedian telling smutty jokes while surrounded by scantily dressed bimbos. Rather predictably, it was a far greater hit in the States.

Simon and Who?

I can guarantee there'll be a couple of albums in your mum and dad's collection that you won't be borrowing... ever. Simon and Garfunkel might be amongst them. They were a 'right on' American singing duo who made a few albums that just about everyone in the world bought. Their most famous song, 'Bridge Over

Troubled Water', recorded in 1970, seemed to embody the wishy-washy hippy-dippy phase so many young people seemed to be going through.

The Power of Punk

In December 1976, the notorious punk band the Sex Pistols were the first rock group to utter the F-word on telly, causing a sensation. They split up after their bass player, a charming lad called Sid Vicious, faced charges of murdering his girlfriend in New York. Their demonic, no-holds-barred 'music' was guaranteed to upset middle-class mums and dads. Unfortunately, what had appeared to be a challenge to the values of modern society was actually a damp squib. It turned out later that they were just a bunch of kids who had allowed themselves to be manipulated by others solely for the money. As a symbol of how tame their 'anarchic' leader, Johnny Rotten (real name John Lydon), has become, he allowed himself to be one of the C-list stars on that ghastly programme *I'm a Celebrity, Get Me Out of Here!* in 2004. Hopefully, that's the last we'll see of him.

1980s

Charles Weds

Poor nineteen-year-old posh girl Diana Spencer made the mistake of her life when she married our Prince Charles. As history now reveals, he was really in love with someone else, but had to be seen to do the right thing. Either way, the great British public loved the ceremony, as they always do. It has been said that whenever the economy is in a mess, give 'em a war or a royal wedding.

Rubik's Cube

In 1980, the world went crazy over an infuriating little puzzle. It was in the form of a cube, made up of individual cubes with different-coloured faces that had to be manipulated so that each of its six sides displayed a single colour. Most of them, like mine, ended up being flung at anyone (usually under twelve) who managed to do it.

Ripping Yarns

As killers go, Peter Sutcliffe, nicknamed the Yorkshire Ripper, was pretty spectacular. This rather ordinary-looking lorry driver with a bad moustache murdered and mutilated thirteen women. When he was arrested in 1981, he claimed that he was insane and didn't know what he was doing, but the court did not agree. I don't know about you, but murdering and then cutting up a load of women seems pretty whacko to me.

American Soap

The most popular TV series in the eighties came from America and described the day-to-day goings on of a ludicrously loaded, dysfunctional Texas oil family. The way they carried on in *Dallas* made the average British family quite grateful they weren't rich. When the principal character, J R Ewing, got shot, it was even relayed on the TV news.

Fearful Fashion

The eighties were to see one of the most sensationally bad eras in fashion – and most of it could be blamed on the States. *Dynasty* (the rather slutty offspring of *Dallas*) promoted big hair, big fingernails, big shoulder pads and a kind of glitzy glamour that had women looking like overdressed, diamond-encrusted Barbie dolls. The men were not much better. It was the era of candy-coloured luminous socks and pale T-shirts worn under pastel suits with the sleeves rolled up. Worst of all, we saw the introduction of the ghastly mullet hairstyle . . . and that was just the grown-ups!

Teenage girls wore short ra-ra and puffball skirts, stonewashed jeans with enormous trainers, leg warmers, and loads and loads of bright colours. The boys sported earrings, leather bracelets, jean jackets with the collars turned up . . . and red braces.

The Iron Lady

There is no one person in the last fifty years more likely to cause violent arguments between your parents and their mates. Margaret Thatcher became the first female prime minister of this country and the population either loved her or hated her. An almost fanatical Conservative, she pulled Britain's economy out of the doldrums and by so doing made the already better-off people (her main supporters) even more so. Her great claim to fame was getting us into and 'winning' a nasty little war with Argentina in 1982 over the barely populated (apart from sheep) Falkland Islands. Many believed the hopelessly one-sided and terribly bloody conflict should never have bloody happened. She was finally deposed in 1990 to the relief of just about everyone, including her followers. Now a very old but not very dear lady, history has not been kind to her and these days many who once supported her keep very quiet if her name ever comes up in conversation.

Live Aid

While world politicians dithered around trying to decide what to do about the tens of thousands of Ethiopians starving to death due to civil war in 1985, Irish pop star Bob Geldof decided to go it alone, putting together the forerunner to 2005's Live 8 concert, Live Aid. Two Live Aid rock concerts were held – one in London and the other in Philadelphia – starring many of the day's leading singers. Together with the single 'Do They Know It's Christmas?', Geldof raised over £40 million. The world's leaders had very red faces that year. Geldof was later knighted by the British Establishment.

The Channel Tunnel

The last person (apart from our boy Brunel) to attempt a tunnel under the English Channel was Napoleon – not to help Anglo-French relations, I might add, but to invade us (as his predecessor William had once done some time back rather more successfully by going over the sea). The go-ahead was given for the Channel Tunnel (or 'Chunnel') on January 20th 1986 and the French and British tunnellers met in the middle in December 1990. Mind you, we still don't get on any better with them.

Yuppies

The term Yuppy (Young Urban Professional) was born in the eighties, as young people in the City made more money than was remotely decent. The 'Big Bang' as it was called occurred in 1986 when the stock exchange was deregulated, allowing anyone with a few quid and a fast tongue to make a killing in stocks and shares. And, oh boy, did they ever! The inflated stock market itself crashed in 1987 and the price of second-hand Porsches tumbled owing to a sudden glut.

Salman Rushdie

If there really is one thing you don't want to do where Muslims are concerned, it's write a novel making fun (allegedly) of their holy book the Koran. Following the publication of *The Satanic Verses* in 1989, the Iranian leader Ayatollah Khomeini issued an order to all Muslims to murder Rushdie if they had half a chance. In 1998 the Iranian government vowed not to put the *fatwa* (religious ruling) into effect, although there is still a reward promised from the Ayatollah for his murder.

End of an Era

On November 10th 1989, the infamous Berlin Wall that separated East Germany from West was torn down. The resulting pieces of the twenty-eight mile wall, built twenty-eight years earlier, was hacked to pieces by delirious souvenir hunters. Suddenly, thousands of East Germans, forced to suffer the strictures of communist oppression, could cross freely. And so they did – in their thousands!

1990s

Queen Dies

In 1991, Freddie Mercury, the singer with the rock band Queen, became the latest and most famous person to die from the dreaded AIDS disease. Like them or hate them, Queen became legendary after his tragic death. Suddenly the British public realised that what the doctors had been saying was true. The AIDS epidemic had virtually no boundaries.

Raving It Up

Suddenly there was something else for parents to worry about in Britain. Impromptu parties, fuelled by drugs and more drugs, began to spring up all over the country in fields and warehouses, wherever large numbers of young

people could congregate. Raves were virtually uncontrol-
lable as no one, especially the police, could predict where
they would spring up next. The 'E' culture was born.

Mad Cows

You must have heard of Mad Cow Disease: Bovine
spongiform encephalopathy (try saying that with a
mouthful of toffees). The disease made the poor creatures
look completely bonkers, waving their heads around
and staggering like they were drunk. Vets discovered
that cows, being normally vegetarian, had been fed on
minced-up sheep meat and bone (because it was cheap
protein). All this might have seemed bad enough, but in
1996, some bright spark made the connection with
humans who had eaten infected beef and had begun
dying of something called Creutzfeldt–Jakob disease or
CJD. Beef was boycotted in restaurants, supermarkets
and schools, which crippled Britain's beef industry to
the tune of £75 billion. That taught the farmers not to
meddle with the natural order of things.

Lady Di-es

In 1992, writer Andrew Morton penned a book about
Prince Charles's then wife, Princess Diana, which
proved something everyone suspected: that the royal

family were no better than the rest of us when it came to having grubby skeletons in their silk-lined cupboards.

Poor Diana spent the last few years of her life frantically trying to find where she fitted in, much to the joy of our appalling tabloid press who made her life a misery. Many say the press were directly responsible for her tragic death in 1997 when they chased her car through a Paris tunnel, causing it to crash into one of the supports.

Diana, Princess of Wales, will be remembered as a stylish, well-meaning (if sometimes misunderstood) fashion icon who simply met the wrong man at the wrong time. The royal family, anxious to push the whole affair under the carpet, ended up with extremely red faces when the British public showed their love of the young princess by piling up literally thousands of farewell bouquets outside their precious palace.

INDEX

INDEX

www.piccadillypress.co.uk

☆ The latest news on forthcoming books

☆ Chapter previews

☆ Author biographies

☆ Fun quizzes

☆ Reader reviews

☆ Competitions and fab prizes

☆ Book features and cool downloads

☆ And much, much more . . .

Log on and check it out!

Piccadilly Press